Acclaim for C.

"There are tens of thousands of gay, lesbian, bisexual and transgender Americans who are still victims of religion based bigotry. They grow up hearing the untruth that homosexuality is a sickness to be healed and a sin to be forgiven. There will never be enough autobiographies like James Helmuth's *Crossing the Bridge* that demonstrate dramatically the tragic consequences of these untruths but at the same time tell the truth from a deeply personal perspective.

After a dramatic retelling of his own struggle to self acceptance, Helmuth announces to the world that he is gay, that he is proud, and that God loves him without reservation. There is no greater truth for the victims of untruth and Helmuth's autobiography proclaims that truth loud and clear."

The Rev. Dr. Mel White, Founder of Soulforce, Inc. and
Author of *Stranger At The Gate* and *Religion Gone Bad*

*   *   *   *

"*Crossing the Bridge* is a courageous memoir by a psychologist who has lived two lives, as a devoted husband for twenty-two years, and the father of two children, and as a gay man enjoying a stable and loving relationship with another man. This is the story of how Dr. James Helmuth grew up within the painfully narrow confines of the Mennonite religion and nearly took his own life in the process of discovering and living his true gay identity.

Unsparingly honest, this memoir reads often like a mystery story, sometimes like a tender recreation of the past — always as a poignant, bittersweet narrative of a boy becoming a man…and a man becoming his true self."

Joseph Dispenza, author of
God On Your Own and *The Way of the Traveler*

*   *   *   *

"Jim Helmuth's *Crossing the Bridge* tells the story of a Mennonite boy becoming a free gay man creating his own kind of family, faith, and love of life. What distinguishes Helmuth's story and gives it universality is how Helmuth, in finding his own way, finds his own voice but leaves no one he loves behind. While Helmuth never dismisses the pain of others along the way, or his own, he shows in this memoir how we must all achieve freedom or our lives become impossible. I suspect you will come to love the man and his unique voice; his journey belongs to us all."

Thomas Dukes, Professor of English, The University of Akron
and author of *Baptist Confidential* and *Sugar Blood Jesus*

* * * *

"I am the oldest of James' family of origin. We are six children - four boys and two girls. I encouraged Jim to write this memoir once I knew he was considering doing that. I bear witness to Jim's honesty, openness, and willingness to finally claim who he always was and is now. Jim loved life enough to travel a difficult and painful journey to be free. He is living into and out of that reality with joy and meaning. He maintains positive relations with all in his family and his siblings who are open to that. Jim did not ask me to write an endorsement but I offered to do it and he accepted. I love and appreciate him very much and have been blessed by having his partner Rich as a part of my life and a part of the Helmuth clan."

David, Jim's eldest brother

Crossing the Bridge

From Mennonite Boy to Gay Man

JAMES L. HELMUTH

iUniverse, Inc.
New York   Bloomington

Crossing the Bridge
From Mennonite Boy to Gay Man

iUniverse books may be ordered through booksellers or by contacting:

iUniverse
1663 Liberty Drive
Bloomington, IN 47403
www.iuniverse.com
1-800-Authors (1-800-288-4677)

Because of the dynamic nature of the Internet, any Web addresses or
links contained in this book may have changed since publication and
may no longer be valid. The views expressed in this work are solely those
of the author and do not necessarily reflect the views of the publisher,
and the publisher hereby disclaims any responsibility for them.

ISBN: 978-1-4401-8846-6 (pbk)
ISBN: 978-1-4401-8848-0 (cloth)
ISBN: 978-1-4401-8847-3 (ebk)

Printed in the United States of America

iUniverse rev. date: 11/16/2009

Dedication

This memoir is dedicated to my partner, Richard Shirey. His unconditional love, loyalty and support over these last twenty years has grounded me so I could find my joy and become who I truly am. This story is not only my story, it is our story for it would not have been possible if Rich had not been by my side every step of the way. For his love, loyalty and wise guidance, I will be forever grateful.

Acknowledgments

I want to thank Roberta Showalter Kreider of Sellersville, Pennsylvania, who in her eighty-three years, has been a valiant witness to God's amazing love and the Jesus Way of acceptance of all of God's lesbian-gay-bisexual-transgendered children into the family of faith. It was she who encouraged myself and other gay people within the Mennonite and Church of the Brethren faiths to tell our stories by editing and compiling them into three published volumes. I am honored to call her my friend and mentor, a Mennonite saint.

I want to thank my book coach, Joseph Dispenza, for his wisdom, editorial guidance and constant encouragement in this project from start to finish. He continued to believe in the value of my story even when I doubted it.

I want to thank Dr. Tom Dukes for his willingness to read the manuscript several times and give frank advice on its form and content. His friendship and encouragement were so important especially this last winter of 2008.

I want to thank Jill Schwartzman, Senior Editor at Random House, for reviewing this manuscript and making excellent suggestions for presentation of the material.

And, most of all, I want to thank my former wife Carolyn, my daughter Jennifer and my son Leif for being such a vital part of my life journey. Each of them, in their own way, encouraged me to write this story even though it was revealing a part of their life journey as well.

Contents

Introduction

The Crossing

Greenwich Road is an unremarkable road that connects the cities of Norton and Wadsworth in northeast Ohio. Along that ordinary road is an ordinary bridge that crosses over an ordinary busy four-lane highway, Route 21.

As I rode my Honda Nighthawk 550 motorcycle along Greenwich Road one spring evening in 1988, something was troubling me very deeply. This evening I did not stop at a park to be quiet and meditate. I was far too angry. I was struggling, without success, to calm conflicting emotions about who I was and what changes I needed to make in my life. Pressure was building from within and I was becoming more and more desperate.

Since it was a cool evening, I was wearing my jeans and the black leather riding jacket I loved so much. It was ironic that I also wore my safety helmet in case of an accident, because an "accident" is exactly what I contemplated. There was a bridge several miles up ahead of me, a bridge I had been thinking about for several days.

I could crash into the side of that bridge and end this miserable life. I imagined I would go over the bridge railing and drop to the busy highway below and be hit by a car or truck. An unfortunate accident! It would be fatal. But my pain and turmoil would be over. I would be at peace and my molecules could be transmuted into the soil or air. My life energy, my being, would continue in some way because energy can never be destroyed, only transmuted.

Yes, I knew it would be a selfish thing to do and cause tremendous pain to my family. But the secret I carried inside was becoming too painful to bear. No one knew or would ever need to know my secret. I've got to end this painful existence. The guilt of my secret life was bearing down on me heavier each passing day. I couldn't carry this heaviness any longer. Reason and concern for others were giving way to the heaviness of my burden. I was trapped with no good options.

I surmised that my family and friends would grieve and make up their meanings of my death. Some would likely say, "God knows best" or "it must have been his time" or something else equally trite. But no one would have to find out about the real me or the truth I carried inside. Yes, my family and friends would grieve and be troubled but eventually go on with their lives.

At forty-four I had it all: a good wife, two beautiful children, a loving extended family, a successful private practice in counseling psychology and the high regard of peers. How could I be suicidal? How could I, Dr. Helmuth, who helps depressed and suicidal people choose life over death, be so very close to ending my own life?

My family loved me and cared about me: that is, they loved the person they thought I was. They knew the good boy "Jimmy" as my siblings called me, the "St. James" as I was known by peers at church, the college graduate, the responsible husband and father, and the Ph.D. psychologist.

They knew my roles, achievements, and my facade. But they did not know my authentic self because I did not know it, or at least was not willing then to tell anyone what I sensed inside. I only had a vague sense of being different from other boys in my family and community. Later as my awareness became clearer, I felt I had no choice but to hide and repress it.

Would they love me if they knew the secret feelings I had carried inside? Could they accept me as I am and not as they assumed I was? Would they judge me and even abandon me? It was a risk I did not want to take. Wouldn't it be better to die physically than keep enduring this living death?

My mind raced and my heart pounded as the bridge was getting closer and closer. I had to decide. I had put off this decision for too long. I had a fear of death. But, I had an even greater fear of life. I was afraid of living with the presumed rejection from loved ones, peers and clients if they knew my secret.

But in my darkest hour, there was something I think could best be called "grace" —even "amazing grace." I can't really explain it, nor do I need to. Whatever the name, it was something even more powerful and motivating than the fear and need for pain avoidance. At a profound level, I felt I was accepted and loved by the Source of life just as I was, without conditions. I wanted to live and not just exist.

Ever since I can remember I had a strong longing to become fully and completely who I was. I longed to live fully and freely regardless of how others defined me, to live my truth, to sing my song, and yes, to color outside the lines! That innate desire to live honestly welled up inside me, and I sped quickly over that bridge to the other side. I was shaking and trembling. Tears clouded my vision so much I could hardly see the road.

I quickly found a place to pull off the road and stop my motorcycle. No sooner did the bike engine stop than a flood of tears, anguish and joy opened and released. I hid my face in my sweatshirt and cried audibly for several minutes. I struggled to regain composure but there was wave after wave of anguished sobbing.

Oh my God, it hurts so badly! What is this pain in my gut? Something has been ripped out. It feels good and yet hurts. I sat there awhile in confusion. What was gone—was it shame? Was it fear? Was it self-loathing? I didn't know. But, something was released inside me. I was glad it was gone. After awhile, I was able to start breathing normally again, as the sobbing stopped.

I wondered if my pain was real or "just psychological," so I pressed on my abdomen and it literally hurt more—my gut was literally tender and remained so for two or three days afterward. It was a physical and emotional change.

The gravel I was sitting on was cold and hard, but I sat there awhile longer anyway thinking about what had just happened. I felt relieved and yet extremely vulnerable. As I blotted up my tears with the gray cotton sweatshirt under my leather jacket, I felt a tender painfulness just below my stomach. It was as if something had been surgically removed from inside me. It left an empty space that was raw and tender. I put the palm of my right hand over the hurt and breathed slowly and deeply. The pain started to ease and the tightness relaxed.

I could linger no longer. It was getting colder outside, and a little wind was starting to chill me to the bone. I had to get back home: my wife and kids might begin to worry where I was and if I had been in an accident. If they only knew, they would be shocked indeed. It scared me to think of how close I came to ending it all. I decided not to tell anyone what had happened. The feelings were too raw and fresh to talk about.

When I got home my kids were upstairs in their rooms and Carolyn was on our long over-stuffed orange sofa, watching TV in the family room. Johnny Cash and June Carter Cash were singing "Ring of Fire," with the words, "and it burns, burns, burns—like a ring of fire, like a ring of fire!" I was feeling my own kind of fire. A fire that was burning away the old hypocrisy and self doubt. It was clearing a space for a new life, a more authentic expression of me. It was burning away the phony walls I had constructed to feel safe.

I suspect Carolyn noticed the redness in my eyes when I came through the family room from the garage but she said nothing and I am glad she didn't. I was not ready to talk to her or anyone about what had just happened. I needed to be with myself, alone.

We had a dark brown Lazy Boy chair in the living room that I loved to relax on in the evenings. I sat on that chair and reclined it fully. I pulled our brown heavy quilted comforter over me for warmth and privacy. It felt very comforting. I lay there quietly for about forty-five minutes before taking a bath and retiring for the evening.

This day was a milestone in my life journey. This day I had chosen life over death. I had chosen to be honest and to live life from a wonderful, loving, peaceful consciousness that was and is my authentic being and my birthright. In a strange way it did seem as though I was starting to live a new life. The decision to live only took an instant. Living it out has taken a lifetime.

I knew the game was over. I had to stop the lying and pretense. I would face my fears and feelings. This would bring big changes for others and myself. I did not know how big those changes would be or how those I loved would respond, but I decided that I would no longer allow how others might respond to keep me in this hellish prison I had just left.

That spring evening, as the earth was warming and coming alive and daffodils and tulips bloomed, something new and beautiful began to spring forth and bloom inside. I began a journey of healing my divided life. I began a journey with no certain destination in mind, except to love and accept myself as I am and to live more honestly. Instead of living for others, I would live with them as best I could. It would take tremendous courage to stay the course but I chose to do it. It felt right.

It would take many years and many dead end streets for me to find the courage to give up the divided life, to stop punishing myself and blaming others for my situation in life.

Chapter One

Birth—Just Fine The First Time

I was born in our farm home near Alliance, Ohio, on a winter morning in January, at about 9:45 a.m. I was mother's fourth surviving son and sixth child. My oldest brother had died of Spina Bifida five days after he was born.

I remember living on the "Supler" farm as we called it. We called it that because Mr. Supler had owned it before us. I remember that I slept in a crib in my parents' bedroom. I also recall exactly where the rooms were and where each of my siblings slept. I was told at times that I was too young to remember those details but that is not true. Those early memories at age two were confirmed later by my parents and siblings.

When I was two and a half years old, there was a defining moment in my life. A man came around to our house periodically to sell Raleigh products for the home. These included products like "pink medicine" for stomach upsets as well as some cooking ingredients like pure vanilla. His car was parked in our driveway. I was playing behind his car. When he backed out of the driveway to leave, he did not see me. His car backed over me but the tires did not run over me.

I was screaming, most likely more from fear than pain. The Raleigh man pulled me out from under the car, picked me up and carried me toward the house. Mother ran out of the house to meet him and clutched me to her breast.

1

She scared me even more as she cried hysterically, clutching me in her arms and running into the house to clean my wounds.

"Why wasn't anyone watching little James? I told you to watch him! Is he ok? He could have been killed! Oh my! I can't believe it. He's not hurt much! Just some scratches and bruises. It's a miracle!" I was only bruised and scraped up by the cinders in the driveway. I was indeed ok.

"I always said, God must have been with James that day and spared his life for some reason," my mother would say when retelling this story throughout my childhood. I didn't like hearing her say that. I wondered what that meant.

I was born and raised in a Mennonite home. This religion taught that God was very involved in our day to day lives and circumstances. Events like the car backing over me were not seen to be random or happenstance. They had some meaning and often some message from God. I eventually figured out that God sparing my life must mean one of two things: I was to become a minister or a missionary. Unfortunately, I did not like either idea. Even though I had a keen sense of spiritual awareness through nature, I did not want it to be my identity or vocation.

This story, as interpreted by my mother, made me feel very special and valued, but I did not like being controlled or pressured by anyone.

Sometimes cousins or peers from my church group would say that I was going to be a minister or missionary. I defensively resisted this suggestion and would protest that I was not going to be a minister. Instead, I was going to be a school teacher or professor. I did not know what a psychologist was at that time or I likely would have chosen that.

I wondered what meaning my mother and others would have given to the car event if the tires of the Raleigh man's car had run over me and killed me or severely crippled me. Would God have been held responsible for that also? I doubt it. "He" always seemed to have a "get out of jail" card.

God, who supposedly controlled every detail of our lives, got credit for sparing my life, but He would never be held responsible if He had ended it. I was told this God was usually compassionate, loving and knew what was best for us and we should never, ever doubt Him, or be angry with him.

But, this God could also be wrathful and send us to hell if we disobeyed him. It didn't make sense to me. In my upbringing, it didn't matter if something did not make sense; I was to just accept whatever the church taught anyway because the truth was revealed in scripture and by the ministers.

Even before I could count to three, I was being defined and manipulated by religion and others intentions and ideas for me. Before I could speak a full sentence, I was told who I was and what I would likely do in life. I had the audacity to believe I should have some say in this matter. I was always on the defensive to explain why I was not going to be a "minister" as was suggested by others. This added to my difficulty in finding a boy self that I could feel good about.

From early childhood on I was told I needed to be re-born and I believed that sincerely. I "accepted Christ" at age eleven and had a sense of relief at being forgiven of my sins. Yet this experience did not magically change my whole worldview or my behaviors. It was my experience of my immediate and extended family that shaped me.

The people who gave me food, shelter and love taught me about a God in the sky who loved us but who also would judge us and punish us when we sin. I assumed these people were absolutely right. After all, they were older and bigger and seemed to be so certain about how things were. Not until later in life did I seriously question this programming.

I learned faith at suppertime. Our wooden table had four legs and was oval-shaped. There was always a pretty flowery oilcloth draped over it so food spills could be easily wiped up. Dad sat at the west end of the oval and mother was immediately to his left. My younger sister was in a high chair next to mom, then my older sister Barb usually sat next to her. My older brothers were next starting with the oldest down to me, the youngest of the boys. I liked sitting next to my father because he was always calm and kind. And, I knew my brothers would not tease me if I were sitting next to dad.

Once the salad, meat and vegetables were on the table, Mother put on her mesh prayer covering and read the Bible reading assigned for that day, plus a short reading of the meaning of the scripture. She would sometimes make a few short comments on what she read. Then each of us at the table who were old enough to speak, were asked to say a Bible verse from memory. This was not difficult because we were often asked to memorize verses for our Sunday School or Summer Bible School classes. We went around the table clockwise. And the unspoken rule was you were not supposed to repeat a verse already given. When it was my father's turn to say a verse, he would often say "all things work together for good, to those who love the Lord." (Romans 8:28 KJV) I have found that to be true.

To be funny, if my dad was away, my next oldest brother or I would sometimes say, "Jesus wept" which is the shortest Bible verse we knew. Just two words. We usually got a glare or stare from mom but nothing more was said. If he was present, my father would then fold his arms, we all had to close our eyes and bow our heads. Then dad began to pray.

In his prayer, he always prayed "for those less fortunate than us" and those who were "sick and afflicted." He would also remember the "bereaved and the shut-ins." Dad always expressed gratitude for what we had. Then he would lead us as we said The Lord's Prayer in unison. My father had an intrinsic faith in God that was evident by the life he lived and how he prayed.

Dad repeatedly used certain phrases in his prayers each time he prayed. I can remember many of them to this day. It was not the words dad said, but the tone and sincerity with which he said them that communicated a faith in God that was real and personal. Dad was a man of few words but his deeds spoke eloquently. He was kind and humble. He seldom spoke negatively of anyone.

I was the fifth surviving child in a family of six. When I was born, a play was already going on in my family. What would my role be in this Helmuth family? How could I help? I wanted to be the best little boy I could be.

As a boy of five, I liked helping my mother in the kitchen and with housework. I noticed how tired she often seemed. She was so busy with raising us six children I wanted to help her in any way I could. I had a clear sense that mother had wanted me to be a girl so I could help her with her work. I had three older brothers to help dad with the farm.

When I was age five and a half my younger sister Carol was born into our family. At about age six, I started to rock her in a small white rocking chair. This cute little child rocker was covered with a white vinyl material and had brown wooden rockers. I would put it near the heat register for warmth and sang and rocked my little sister to sleep. I felt proud that I could sometimes get her to sleep when she was fussy. Mother would praise me for being so helpful.

Even though she was just a baby, Carol claims she can remember these times. She recalls these times as being very nurturing to her. There has always been a close bond between she and I even to this day. We share and seem to understand each other.

I was taken to church every Sunday morning and most Sunday evenings. There was also a mid-week prayer service.

Sunday morning in my local Mennonite church typically started with two songs sung in four- part harmony without accompaniment. A prayer, announcements, scripture readings, a sermon of twenty to forty-five minutes, another song, or two, another prayer and dismissal. The church sanctuary was divided with two sets of hard wooden benches. Women sat on one side and men on the other.

During the long church services, we children could sit on either side of the sanctuary but usually sat with our mothers or aunts. The women were to all wear dresses or skirts below the knee, have their hair long, wear a prayer veiling and be quiet. The men could wear pretty much what they wanted to with no restrictions on hair. Unlike the Amish, beards were OK but not encouraged or required.

The theme of the sermons would usually be something like this: man was an awful sinner from birth. He disobeyed God and engaged in sins of pride and arrogance. Of the various sins, sexual sins got much more rap than others, or at least I remembered them more. God was very angry with man and was going to send us all to hell if we did not repent and change our ways. But he reconsidered and sent Jesus to die on the cross to appease his anger. So be glad Jesus got you off the hook.

But to stay off the hook you had better live a holy and chaste life or you could get it anyway (sent to hell). No one explained how human sacrifice pleases God or why that was necessary except that the Jewish people used to kill perfect goats and sheep to please him and they believed it would make God happy, because it showed they were sorry for their sins. That might have made sense to the Jewish people but made no sense to me as a child growing up in the 1950's.

Once we accepted Christ, usually at about age 12, we were then saved and became part of his holy church. We were to live clean and pure lives to please him. We were to look and be different from the sinful world. Yes, to be a proper Christian sister, Mary was to wear a dress below the knee and not cross her legs. She was to have long hair hanging down or rolled up on top of her head and covered with a prayer covering. She might feel proud of her modesty and gossip about the others who did not look as spiritual as she but that was not discussed much. One could easily tell who was a "true" Christian woman or not. It was much more difficult to tell true Christian men because we wore pants and shirts just like the world.

The assumption in all of this theology was that we were bad, sinners, shameful people and we were born that way. We needed to be saved from our condition. This is easy to believe and seems to make sense because there is ample evidence of evil all around us. If something bad happened to someone, that was evidence that they were sinful and being punished by God. And God allowed the bad to happen to get them to repent and come to him.

It was occasionally said we were "born in the image of God." But that was seldom explored or considered very seriously. Even as a very young child I had a sense that I was a spirit, a being from somewhere else. I had a sense that I was born ok. My many walks in nature led me to feel a natural closeness to my Source of life. Before I joined the Mennonite religion, I sensed I was a spiritual being and precious.

But as my mind here on earth was imprinted with the agenda of people around me and the struggles of life, I forgot this being I was and began to fear. This beautiful consciousness I had known slowly faded into beliefs of being bad, sinful, shameful and inadequate.

Chapter Two

Moon Over Swallen Road

Between the paved roads of Route 153 and Georgetown Road, three and a half miles east of Louisville in northeast Ohio, is a three-mile dirt and gravel road named for a Mr. Swallen, who owned the farm at the corner. When there was a dry spell in the summertime, our traveling down this dirt road in a car would stir up so much dust that one could barely see the person next to you in the car. My family lived on a farm two and one half miles down this dirt road. In winter, snow often drifted Swallen Road shut by the west to east winter winds that piled the snow up to four feet high.

It was a very cold Sunday in January of 1953. I was nine years old. My parents, three brothers and two sisters had been to morning church services. The night before, I had invited a second cousin to bring his train set over after church that Sunday and put it together with mine to make a nice layout. After lunch we played with the trains most of the afternoon. Then it was time to milk the cow, gather the eggs and feed the thousands of chickens we had on our farm. After dinner some of the family and myself went back to church for the evening service.

After church services and visiting with friends for forty-five minutes, it was time to go home. Dad drove our 1949 four-door Dodge car home from our Mennonite church meeting. Mom was in the front seat holding my younger sister. One of my three brothers and my older sister were beside me in the back seat. I was by the window. I always liked sitting by the car window at night so I could look out and see the stars and the moon.

At church that night, everyone met in the sanctuary for a hymn and a prayer. The adults stayed upstairs to hear their second sermon of the day, usually by whichever of our two ministers did not preach that morning, while children my age were hustled to the basement for our own classes. This evening we were told stories of our Mennonite missionaries in Africa and their work there to help the people dig wells for water but also to win them to Christ. In learning about far away lands and different cultures, I was impressed by how big and diverse our world was.

But that cold night coming home from church in our car, I was not thinking about how big our world was. I was thinking how very small our world was. I looked up and saw the full winter moon high in the sky. I looked to see if there might be a man in the moon. I wondered if the moon was perhaps the face of Jesus. Maybe Jesus wasn't in heaven and instead lived on the moon, if so he would be closer than heaven. I heard some joking that the moon might be made of green cheese. I was quite sure there was no man, cheeses, or Jesus on that beautiful sphere. But I was very curious about what might actually be there.

As our car traveled down Swallen Road toward our farm home that night, I remember a strange sense that I could, for a brief time, leave the car to see our beautiful earth as the tiny speck it is from the perspective of someone standing on the moon. I was in absolute awe that our planet was so small and seemingly insignificant. I had learned in science class that our earth was a planet circling the sun. It is one of billions of stars in the universe and the universe was billions of years old. I had learned that there were many other galaxies out there and that our earth was certainly not the center of the universe.

That winter night I began to question more what I was being taught in church: If God were a man-like being out there or up there in heaven some place, how could he keep track of all our thoughts, feelings, and behaviors? Why did *He* (male, of course) want to judge and punish us? How could any one of us specks on this small speck of earth know the truth for all? And to claim to know absolute truth seemed to me to be the epitome of arrogance.

Supposedly "we Mennonites" had *the* true faith. We were to go out and convert the rest of the world to our faith. Starting as children and continuing to adulthood, we heard about Mennonite mission work in other countries.

Sometimes missionaries on furlough would speak and show slides at our church, as they would awe us with successes of helping the poor in third world countries and in converting them from godless heathenism to Christ. I always thought it would be nice to be a missionary on furlough, except I would have to be a missionary first. My oldest brother became an ordained Mennonite minister and he and his wife and children were missionaries to Puerto Rico for 15 years. The family didn't need another missionary, fortunately.

But in my home and church, there was less concern about the unbelievers in the community than there was about the Catholics. They were especially seen as wrong because of their belief in the pope and worshiping the Virgin Mary. They were dangerous, I was told, because they wanted to convert us if they could. Some of our young Mennonite men married Catholic girls and more often than not converted to the Catholic faith. They were the competition.

Our local Catholic church in Louisville was a huge building that looked very dark and scary to me. The limestone exterior was a dark blackish color from years of weathering. As a young boy, I was afraid to walk past this building for fear that a priest might run out and grab me and make me Catholic. (I had no idea then about the priest/altar boys abuse going on, or I might have had good reason to be concerned.) Maybe part of me secretly wished a priest had grabbed me!

Even as a child I noticed good things happen to criminals and bad things happen to good and loving people. What's that about? The explanation that if something bad happened to you God was calling you to repent did not make sense to me. It was too simplistic. It seemed to me that if this was how our God was, He was mean, capricious and manipulative. Not someone I could love or trust.

Growing up Mennonite had its good and bad parts. Within my local Mennonite church there were divisions and infighting. Some clans supported the more conservative older bishop while other clans supported the more liberal youth minister. The battle line was not between young and old but between biological families. Most of the members in our church could be traced to three or four family groups. This division came up at most every discussion of church matters and at times of voting for church leaders. We were peace-loving pacifists who would not pick up a sword but would use our tongues to verbally attack each other, and smile while doing so.

And yet, if any member in the church was in need from fire, illness or accident everyone would pitch in to help share the load no matter what it took. There was a safety net below us that most all of us felt. Sometimes help was given freely to neighbors who were not members of our church. Help was also given for new projects or buildings in other countries particularly after a disaster. Two of my uncles who were carpenters gave several months of time to help the people of Honduras rebuild after a devastating hurricane.

Even though I was only a child, I was tuned into the larger picture of our world situation and politics. I was concerned about the arms race and the threats of violence and war. Mrs. Fry, my fourth grade teacher, told our class about the Russians and the missiles they had aimed at us. "There was a bomb with the name of our city on it," she said. I learned the Russians could drop atomic bombs on us at any time. I was very impressionable and lived with this fear of death in my young life until I was in my late teens. I would pray over and over that it would not happen before I could grow up and live my life.

As a young boy, I was also very curious about my body and sex. When I was eleven I attended a boy's week at our church camp. During camp I noticed a book in the bookstore about our bodies and sex. I wanted to read it but did not have the money to buy it during camp. And I was far too shy about sex to have the book in my belongings.

When my parents came to pick me up on the last hot summer evening of camp, I took mother to the bookstore and shyly pointed at the book, asking her to buy it for me. I sensed my mother was interested in me getting this sex information. She bought the book and put it in her purse until we got home. She then gave it to me and I took it downstairs to the tall cherry desk-bookcase with twin glass doors and four shelves and a pull-down desk lid. I pulled open the glass doors, and put my book on a shelf in between some old books. I hid it as if it were some dirty pornography magazine. I had to start somewhere in my sex education and this book was the only one available to me.

On Sunday afternoons, and other times as well, when my parents were busy and my siblings were away, I would quietly sneak down stairs and go to the cherry bookcase. Unfortunately the twin glass doors in front of the books stuck at the top and bottom so they made a little rumbling noise when opened as if to announce, "Someone's in the bookcase." The rumble sound was not very loud but to me I feared someone would surely hear it and inquire as to what I was doing.

I would pull so gently on the doors but they always rumbled. I was so afraid someone would find me reading this book. This paperback book of about a hundred pages of sex information had a yellowish cover, which soon got torn by frequent use.

While this book had some basic and accurate information about sex and procreation, it was sufficiently vague to leave many things unexplained, especially the things I really wanted to know about! I was curious just how the sperm and egg would meet so a woman could get pregnant. The text was void of any discussion of love and passion. It had some Spartan drawings of anatomically correct naked men and women that I would look at over and over while pleasuring myself. The pictures were totally sterile but I had a good imagination.

I was not only curious about the universe without, I was curious about the universe within me. Why do I feel the way I do? Why do I feel so different from my siblings and peers at school and church?

Many gay men tell me that they "always knew" they were gay and recall specific times where that was clear to them, often starting at ages of four or five or even earlier. I did not hear the word gay as referring to sexual orientation until I was about sixteen.

My awareness of feeling different from other boys started at an early age but it wasn't until puberty that I can recall noticing and experimenting with same-sex attraction—-and then I had no context for understanding what was going on with me. Were my more liberal religious beliefs partly a cover for the same-sex feelings I was having that were different from other boys? They may have been. I was convinced both my doubts and my different feelings had to be carefully hidden, particularly the same-sex attractions.

As I walked and worked in nature on our farm near Louisville Ohio, I felt keenly aware of the beauty of our world and the complexity of each living organism. It did seem to me there was some divine intelligence and Source of Life. But I didn't know what to call it then and even now.

Chapter Three
Nails

I would prefer not to have to write this chapter but I must. It is difficult to write about what I am not proud of.

My brother, who was eighteen months older than I, was nevertheless about my same size. As I was growing up, he and I fought constantly over chores and competitive games. It usually got vicious with hitting, kicking and punching until one of us prevailed. Mom would tell us to stop but did not get between us.

Mother was the hardest worker I have ever known. Typically she would get up at 4:30 a.m. to make lunches for us children and my dad. After dad was off to his day job delivering meat to grocery stores in Cleveland, she would prepare meals for the day until it was time to get us children up for breakfast and sent off to school.

Mother once told me that she had felt called to be a missionary but decided instead to marry and raise a Christian family. So her deepest desire was that all of her children would be Christians and serve God.

As I was growing up at home, I would often awaken to sweet music coming from the kitchen downstairs. It was the beautiful voice of my mother singing some of her favorite hymns. Mother was an excellent soprano and would sometimes sing in ladies' or mixed quartets. Mother was usually happy. No one who heard her sing could ever doubt "what a friend we (she) had in Jesus!" She found in Him her strength to go on each day and her joy of living.

With only one heat register for the three bedrooms upstairs where we children slept, it was very cold in winter! On cold mornings it was hard to leave the comfort of a warm bed, a sweat lodge of blankets piled high to keep us warm. But the smell of bacon frying in the big cast iron skillet downstairs helped motivate me to get up and get going anyway.

One Saturday morning, when I was about nine years old, I came down the creaking steps from upstairs one at a time and sat on the bottom step of the landing which opens up into our large country kitchen. Mom was making me a toast and bacon sandwich as she often did. No one else was around. It was just mom and me.

Today, mom was not singing and I wondered why. I waited in silence as I sensed something was wrong. Even the bacon sandwich could not draw me to the table though I was hungry.

Mother stood working at the new lime green porcelain sink my uncle Kenneth had recently installed. Her hair was rolled up tightly around a U-shaped cloth hair roller. She had her checkered brown work apron on that had two big pockets in the front. I could tell mom was upset because she was tearful. She had been crying. I knew something was brewing and it was more than the coffee.

Mother saw me at the landing, looked me in the eye and said, "James, I just don't know what to do with you boys fighting so much! It seems every night you get in a fight about doing the chores. Why can't you and Dale just get along? You can't imagine how much it hurts me to hear you fighting or you wouldn't do it!" I did not answer this time. I had heard this plea before but never when she was so distraught.

Then she leaned and put her head on her left arm and leaned against the upper plywood cupboards where we kept the pink Melmack "every-day" dishes that we got free from redeeming coupons we tore off of hundreds of chicken-feed bags we bought on the farm.

"I just don't understand why God gave me children if he knew I didn't know how to raise them," she lamented and began to cry. I hated to hear her blame God.

I was startled to see mother so upset. A terrible feeling of guilt and shame came over me like an ominous black storm cloud. I didn't know what to do.

13

I felt like running away and hiding. "Stop mother, please! I will be good. I won't fight anymore," I said. But she continued…

"I read where a lady once told her children that every time they fought, they put another nail in her coffin. Then they stopped fighting."

I could stand no more. Not even the bacon sandwich waiting for me could keep me there. I bounded up the stairs two at a time, got under the heavy covers on my bed and wept. I began lamenting, saying to myself "I'm sorry mother I am too much for you. I'm sorry I am so bad. Forgive me for being so terrible! How could I hurt my mother like this? And when she dies it will be my fault! What can I do? I promised myself to try not to fight with Dale anymore. There must never be any more nails!"

But there would be more nails, lots of them.

Fortunately I was not at all considered a bad boy in my school, church and community. I got above-average grades and learned quickly. In 8th grade I was given an award for citizenship, courage and valor. It was a heavy round bronze medal with those words inscribed around the circumference. I polished and cherished that medal for years. Someone saw goodness in me, even courage and honor!

This medal was awarded by the American Legion yearly to the best citizen in the eighth grade class at our school. I thought it was ironic that the American Legion would give the award to a Mennonite boy who was a pacifist. Perhaps those choosing were the only ones who did not know I was Mennonite. After some discussion, my parents left me keep the medal. I kept it in its original box and put it in the big cherry bookcase/dresser with other valuables.

But the biggest challenge I had was to find out just where I belonged in this family. My older siblings were already finding themselves in the world when I came along. I tried to find who I was by picking on and competing with Dale, my brother closest to me in age. It felt like I was put in a play that was already in progress. I was not given a script so I had to find my role by watching closely how others responded to me, and then figure out what my role really was to be in my family.

Sometimes there was positive competition in various sports like ping pong, basketball, wrestling and boxing. I would win my fair share of games. But often I was a very sore loser when I lost. I often could not accept defeat without a big scene. If I lost the ping pong match I would sometimes hurl the paddle at my brother who had to duck to miss it, at times unsuccessfully.

I was very jealous of my brother when he would be invited to a birthday party or other event and I wasn't. Since he was a little older, he naturally got to do some things sooner than I. This would anger me.

I was afraid that I was not OK, I was not enough and that I was not as good or intelligent as others. I sometimes feared I was not really loveable or worthy. I felt this way in spite of getting good grades and being recognized at school and church.

I wrote several drafts of this chapter without including one critical incident. And when I finally wrote about this incident, I initially changed some of the details of the incident so I did not look quite so bad! This shows I still feel a tinge of shame about it. It seemed I remembered only certain details and ignored others. I had to go back and revise my writing of this incident to speak the truth.

Spring was in the air. We were busy preparing the fields for planting corn, wheat and oats. I was twelve and Dale was thirteen and a half. Someone had used our Ferguson 30 tractor in the field to do some harrowing and had left it sitting outside of the shelter. The clouds were becoming darker and foreboding. We could hear thunder in the distance, a storm was coming.

There was a roof over an area between the two corn cribs on our farm and my dad said to put the tractor in there for the night so it would be protected from rain. He didn't say which of us should do it.

Dale and I raced for the tractor. He got there first, jumped on it and drove it between the corn cribs. I tried to jump on as he drove it but couldn't.

I was furious because he won and when he got off the tractor I started a fight by hitting and kicking him as hard as I could. He naturally defended himself and hit back. Just before I ran away, I kicked at him as hard as I could and caught him in the groin. He dropped to the ground like a lead weight and just laid there motionless. He was white as a sheet.

"Oh my God! I killed my brother" I thought. I ran into the house crying and screaming for help. Dad ran out to where my brother was lying on the ground and knelt down by him. I was so ashamed and scared I ran and hid behind the big old pear tree in the yard between the barn and the house. I peered out from behind it to see what was happening. Soon I saw my brother and dad walking through the yard toward the house. I was hugely relieved. My brother was just fine, but I wasn't.

For a few moments, I thought I had killed him, and my body reacted as though I had. I stayed outside awhile until everything had calmed down. I thought sure dad would spank me but he didn't. Perhaps he could see how upset I was. That awful memory left a sensitive wound that I sometimes still feel inside me.

My brother and I have long since reconciled and forgiven each other but it is the trapped shame and guilt that lives on inside in the form of an emotional wound. That incident actually helped me in some ways in that I could see what my anger and rage could do. I was confronted boldly with the reality that my uncontrolled anger could kill. I did not want to kill anyone. That was the worst sin. This incident motivated me to control my temper. I am not completely sure, but I do not recall ever having a physical fight with my brother after that incident.

I became aware of sexual arousal and tension starting around age nine. My early feelings of arousal were for both the same and opposite sex. I sensed somehow that there was something wrong with the feelings of sexual arousal regardless of what they were.

In the middle of one of our fields, close to our farm home on our one hundred acre farm, there was a small hill with a group of four or five trees and a small area of grass. There were two or three gravestones with the family name "Blake" engraved on them. I was told that Mr. Blake, who owned our farm before us, and his wife were buried there. There were also stones collected there from the fields. Since we did rotation farming, that field was sometimes planted with corn and sometimes with wheat or oats. When there was corn there, the graveyard was barely visible.

One fall, when corn was planted in that field, Roy, a neighbor boy several years older than I, asked me to meet him at the graveyard to play after school. Roy was very cute and funny. I liked him a lot. I had fantasized just being alone with Roy. But, when I got to the graveyard Roy was there with Ben, another neighbor boy. I thought we were going to play hide and seek among the cornrows with the graveyard as home base. However, Roy and his friend Ben had other ideas. They rubbed their crotches slowly and asked me if I knew about "wieners" and how they might "get you" if you are not careful. I said, "No, what do you mean?"

They pulled down their jeans and started playing with themselves and laughing. They told me to do the same. I was very hesitant, scared and excited at the same time. I did as they asked. We touched and stroked each other. It felt wonderful and yet I was scared that I had done something bad. I never told anyone about what happened. Even though I was scared and felt guilty, I sneaked away from the farm home and met Roy and Ben there several more times that season to "play" in the cornfield. It was one of my earliest experiences of feeling aroused with others of my same sex.

Those feelings of interest in other boys could never be talked about openly and honestly. In addition to society's taboos, there were religious teachings that reinforced the idea that sex was dirty. Certain words that referred to sex were considered bad or dirty. I started to feel ashamed of my body sensations and to distrust what my body told me felt good.

In Sunday school class at church, I was taught sexual feelings were sinful, except for procreation and marital happiness in a traditional marriage. There were discussions about the sins of "sodomy "and the "sin of Onan (masturbation)." If the Bible labeled these warm, loving and sexual feelings as bad and sinful, then I assumed I was bad for feeling them. This began the alienation from my own body and natural feelings. A negative or "bad boy" self was set up within me that I tried to repress and hide.

For some years between ages six and nine, I had a problem with s-s-s-s-stuttering. Fortunately it was not very severe but it did cause me some embarrassment at home and at school. I was teased about it sometimes and mocked.

Eventually I was able to overcome my stuttering by taking a full breath before starting to speak. It helped so much that my mother told me that she read that those who stutter do so because they are very intelligent and have so much to say they try to talk too fast.

I never researched mom's statement and just accepted it readily because it was useful to me. It does illustrate how a positive interpretation of a problem area can make a huge difference in the emotional effects of a problem on the child.

I wonder how my life might have been different if a similar positive or even neutral meaning had been offered to me regarding my sexual attractions and my felt differences in interests from other boys. If only I had someone to talk with about my feelings and fears. A special someone that would not have labeled those feelings as wrong or bad.

But I had no one to talk with. And by myself, I was not in good company. I was sure I was bad and different. Did other boys have sexual feelings for other boys or men? If they did, they were called sinful, queer, faggots or sissy. The gay word was just starting to be used at this time and had a very negative connotation. Those referred to as gay were not the kind of human beings I could ever be part of in any way. I was in a wilderness, lost and very alone. How could I ever find my way home?

Chapter Four

I'm Just One Of You Guys

Tony Bennett may have left his heart in San Francisco, but I left my wits in Canton, Ohio, just over the brim of that first straight-up hill of my first ever roller coaster. The tracks bottomed out after that first drop and leveled off just a bit as we headed toward a sharp curve and higher elevation.

I heard the coaster car wheels clack against the rail joiners like ticking time bombs ready to go off at any moment. The wooden trestles creaked and shivered with the heavy weight of six linked cars and sixty fools. I was sure I was going to die!

For two weeks, my cousins Lenny and Aaron were trying to persuade me to go on this great roller coaster ride at the Myers Lake Amusement Park in Canton, Ohio. I was very uneasy but so as not to be "chicken," agreed to try it. At twelve, I needed to prove that I was tough and one of the boys. I didn't much like being called "chicken" or "scaredy cat". They already teased me about being a sissy because I liked to cook.

So there I was, in midair, on that first drop, I knew fear as never before in my whole life. I was petrified as I grasped the safety bar so tight my arms ached. I felt moistness in my crotch and hoped to god I hadn't really wet myself. That would be the ultimate embarrassment.

As we climbed toward heaven (or maybe hell) I had just enough time to catch my breath and pray '"Dear Jesus! Please get me off of this ride safely, please…. I promise never ever to go on another one…and I promise not to fight with my brother anymore….pleaszz!"

Before Jesus could answer my proposition we dropped again and jerked to the left—where's my stomach?—hey guys—its back there—I'm not fully here. I'm being dismembered at each drop and curve. "Please Jesus, get me off this thing, now!"

After what seemed like an eternity of more drops, curves and jerks, I felt us slowing down and coming into the end gate station.

"Oh, yes, I made it."

We all had to exit quickly and clear the track. White as a sheet and scared drunk, my rubber legs and I stumbled down the exit ramp to blessed terra firma. Finally I could breathe normally.

As I squeezed my legs together to hide my crotch, Lenny yelled "Hey Jimmy, did you like it? Wasn't that fun? Let's get in line and do it again!"

"Sure guys, of course," I said. I actually thought, "Anyone for the Merry Go Round?" I obviously couldn't say that—so I failed the macho boy test. "No, you guys go ahead, I don't want to wait in that long line again," I said. This time they did not pressure me to join them—and I never ever went on another coaster. Well almost—years later I rode the Corkscrew at Cedar Point but rationalized that it wasn't a true roller coaster because it did not have huge drops.

And the "no fighting with brother promise."—hmm—It might have lasted twelve hours at most.

I know now I was going through the normal struggle to find my identity, my place in the family, but it seemed my older siblings already took all the good roles. My oldest brother, David, went into the ministry. My two other brothers were into sports and later became school teachers. My older sister Barb was in college to be a school teacher, too. I was very impressed with her caring way with children. And my younger sister, Carol had the "baby of the family" slot. Who was "Jimmy"? What was left for him?

Playing sports was highly valued in my immediate and extended family. I was a little above average at some sports and average at others. I was better at individual sports like ping pong and wrestling than team sports. Even though I could play softball and volleyball quite well, I was just not interested very much in sports. In my family that was not accepted, especially for a boy. My older sister was an excellent slugger in softball and she got special kudos for being a good basketball and volleyball player in college.

My siblings and cousins sometimes played softball in the back yard or the pasture near our farm home. One Sunday afternoon in July, it was the kind of hot humid day where any wisp of breeze was welcomed. My cousins Dan and Kenny came to our place to play ball in the front cow pasture by our house. Some of my siblings were there. My brother rounded up some other neighborhood kids so there would be enough for two teams, but they needed more players.

As they were recruiting players, I went in the house to play with my Lincoln Logs because I didn't want to play ball. I was a good hitter but they would sometimes make fun of me if I missed a catch. And besides playing in ninety degree humid weather was not appealing. Since they needed more players, Dan and Kenny set out to find me. When they arrived I was playing in the back living room of my house in front of a fan.

"C'mon Jimmy," Dan said, "play ball with us. We need you!"

"No! I don't want to play. Its too hot!," I yelled.

"Hey Jimmy, You can play third base," Kenny said.

"Are you sure? I will only play third or be the pitcher." I said.

"OK, it's a deal" they said.

I kind of liked playing third base because I was pretty good at ground balls and I could throw to first base easily. I liked pitching even more because I had a strong arm, a good underhand fast ball and fairly good control. They promised third or pitching so I relented and told them I would play.

I played with my Lincoln Logs set a few more minutes just to make them wait and then slowly got up to fulfill the bargain. When I got to the pasture, all the other players were in position, including someone playing third base and someone pitching.

"Hey, I thought you said I could play third base" I said.

'Well, you can. We need someone to stand at third base so we can see where it is, fatso Doug explained. He himself would have made a great third base bag.

"No way!" I screamed, 'I'm not going to be the bag, you tricked me!"

They pleaded and bargained, "please, Jimmy, just for a few innings, then you can pitch, we promise". They just broke one promise, why would I trust them to keep another.

I picked up a dried cow chip and hurled it at them like a Frisbee. Cow chips are fairly brittle but if you are careful, they will fly. "Here, use this for the bag!" I yelled as I ran off to the rock pile…half crying and half laughing as the cow chip broke into pieces when it hit the ground. "Ha ha…serves you right," I yelled. It felt good to release my anger again.

Is it any wonder I hated to play softball when cousins and neighbors got together to play? Family reunions were the worst as they were often held at rural churches or parks with ballfields. I had to be creative to find hiding places so I would not be cajoled into playing sports and getting teased as a result. I sometimes took a long walk so they could not find me.

I felt different from my brothers and especially boy cousins because I was different. And for most any child, different = inferiority. I would much rather put puzzles together and talk about school things with my girl cousins. But since this was not the accepted norm for boys, I was teased about being "a sissy."

My parents bought me an Erector set with an electric motor for my tenth birthday. I was ecstatic. I loved it. Of course I colored outside the lines, so to speak. I did not do many of the projects in the booklet that came with the set. Instead I turned the motor upside down and put wheels on it to make a dune buggy or car! I spent hours playing with that set and kept it through the years.

Evidently, mom and dad did see my interests were different than my brothers and this was their way of showing it. That helped so much. I would rather read, play with my erector set or bake cookies with my girl cousins. I taught myself to type using the correct fingering shown in a book that came with an old Underwood typewriter that my mother bought.

Between ages twelve to fourteen, I got up early on Saturday mornings so I could sneak away on my bike before my siblings were up. I would ride twenty minutes to Aunt Ruby and Uncle Irvin's farm. There I would do housework and baking with my cousin Kaye Jean while my aunt went to town to teach music lessons. My aunt paid me five dollars each week and I liked learning to bake chocolate chip cookies and banana cake.

Usually I could not get away from home without being noticed by my siblings, but I went anyway! I bragged about the money I got and smugly tucked it away in my old mustard jar bank that had the face of a man etched in it. I kept this jar in the big cherry desk bookcase because it had twin glass doors that would help me keep an eye on it. I was frugal and saved for a new bicycle or camera. I also knew I wanted to go to college some day and would need money.

Mother's interpretation of the car accident at age two and a half was partly right. I did feel a sense of having something special to do in life, but it had to do with living out this life journey I had started. I was and am a special soul, unique and precious—just like everyone else!

This is a wonderful paradox. The longing to live out my life fully was very strong. I would sometimes scan the skies when out walking or driving the tractor in the fields to see if there were planes or missiles overhead. I was very frightened if I saw or heard jets in the sky break the sound barrier. I don't recall ever telling anyone of my fear as I was ashamed to be afraid. Boys were to be strong and never cry.

One thing that seemed to set me apart from other children is that I had an unusually keen awareness of how people treated each other and how they treated me. I had always been very aware of the divisions and infighting in my local church. This bothered me because I overheard the anger and frustration my parents felt when they talked to others about our local church. Hearing this also made me very curious about why people felt and acted the way they did toward each other.

At the southeast corner of our five-acre cow pasture, piles of stones surrounded several hickory and walnut trees. The stones were stacked there when we found them in the fields when plowing or harrowing. Over the years, this stone pile grew quite large.

I loved going to the stone pile where I could be completely alone and sit in the shade of those trees. It was cooler there and private. It seemed there was always a breeze blowing through those trees.

There I would talk to myself and the God of my childhood understanding. I would sometimes rail against people I disliked. I would take the rocks and sometimes smash and grind them on each other when angry or frustrated, and that seemed much of the time. One of the people I loved to be angry with was Zack.

Though not his real name, everyone called him "Zack," which was short for Zacchaeus, a man in the New Testament of the Bible who was said to be of short stature. Zack was barely five foot tall. He was a member of my local Mennonite congregation. He had short white hair and was at almost every church service faithfully. Sometimes it might only be Zack and several others at mid-week services.

Zack had a wife and four children. His wife dressed very conservatively which meant that she wore a dress that came down to her shins and had a cape to hide the form of her breasts. Her hair was curled up on a hair roller and she wore the prayer veiling even when not in church. Mennonite ladies who wore their veiling twenty-four--seven supposedly got extra points with the Almighty.

Zack was conservative and zealous in his beliefs. He tried to keep his children in line by not permitting them to do some of the things other youth in our church did. As with most Mennonite youth, some of his children found devious ways to do what they wanted anyway. Some left home as soon as they could find a way to be on their own.

Zack's face was like a gray slate, hard and expressionless. I never saw him smile and he seldom looked anyone in the eye when talking to them. He carried a large Bible which he carried with one finger stuck in between the pages, I suppose so as to not lose his place. He studied his Bible during church services and even during church business meetings. It appeared he was in his own world and not listening at church business meetings. Wrong. He was listening and spoke his mind when opportunity was given. I admired him for even correcting the ministers and bishops at times with his knowledge of the Old Testament.

Zack loved the Old Testament and would expound on some esoteric aspect of the Temple of Israel any time he could. It seemed he read and re-read the Old Testament constantly and tried to live by its teachings.

I disliked Zack because he seemed so negative and conservative. He championed the tired old phrase, "what will this change lead to," and used it to pooh-pooh most new ideas. He seemed afraid that if you give an inch "they" will take a mile. "They" were the liberal influences and practices that were creeping into the church which frightened him. In contrast, I welcomed changes and new ideas because the old ways were far too constricting for me and my generation.

Some years Zack was on the church council which made decisions about church activities and programs. When I was the youth leader and wanted to implement some innovative programs for the youth, Zack was usually against these changes. He could find some scriptural reason to oppose anything new.

In spite of his opposition, some more progressive programs were accepted, particularly in the youth group.

While I was in the youth group, Zack's wife became ill with a terminal illness and died within about six months of the diagnosis. During her illness, my dad and I visited Zack several times. One Sunday evening after the chores were done and we had supper, dad and I stopped by Zack's home for another visit. As we were leaving, Zack had tears in his eyes and started to cry. My heart went out to him. I felt for his pending loss. I felt badly for the family problems and unhappiness he seemed to have. It was good to see that this stone-faced man did not have a stone heart. He could let himself feel his own pain and pending loss and begin to grieve. I felt empathy for this man I had judged so harshly when I could see his humanness and noble intentions.

In sharp contrast with my angry feelings toward various people in my life, I felt a wonderful, calm feeling when in nature. Fall weather was a favorite time of year, as I loved the orange, yellow and red hues of the leaves. Nature accepts you just as you are, there is no judge except the natural order of life and death. I could relax.

In nature I could laugh, cry or be angry. And I was a boy with lots of angry thoughts. I could be in and with my body in a more authentic and natural way when in nature and so I would look for opportunities to go for walks alone.

What happened to this beautiful and loveable boy that came from somewhere to this planet? Where was his natural self? That beautiful little boy got lost in the ego need to be accepted and belong in my family. He learned to repress and deny whatever did not fit into the family values.

But this part of me was not dead—he would respond when in nature and with a few friends. The consciousness of that former realm would come into focus when I saw a beautiful flower or sunset. Walking along the seashore has always brought a special awareness of who I am and that depth from which I came. Deep calls unto deep.

Years later, while journaling about my feelings, I became keenly aware of this alienated child I called my "little boy". This journal entry expresses what I often felt but could not say while growing up.

"I am a little boy. I am a lonely little boy. I am a lonely boy who wants to be held and touched and played with but who is ashamed to ask for what he wants. I am a little boy who feels inferior, who feels guilty for having needs, who feels separate from others. I am a little boy who wants someone to love him for who he is, not for whom he is supposed to be!"

It was a relief to be able to find this part of me as an adult, and to begin to nurture him rather than waiting for someone else to find him and love him. It helped when I could realize that I was not solely responsible for my mom's feelings.

My descent into shame and guilt was not that unusual. While difficult, my childhood was not nearly as violent or dysfunctional as many children experience. My parents and siblings were there for me and loved me as best they could. My problems were caused by my own self-rejection and harsh judging of my own body and feelings.

Karl Marx claimed that religion is "the opiate of the people." There is some truth in his observation. I grasped on to religious explanations and reassurances to quell my fears of death. While I was experiencing a lot of emotional pain about my life at home, being involved in my church helped me feel good about myself. At church, I was accepted and sometimes praised. I could feel superior to my peers and others. And that did soothe my feelings of shame at home, but church and religion did not get to the core of that problem.

Chapter Five

Achieving Sainthood

"You can never eliminate the ego, you only find it lives in a larger house than you thought."

(author unknown)

The summer after I turned eleven years old, several local Mennonite churches set up a pole tent that would hold two or three hundred people for evangelistic revival services. This was a smaller version of what other Mennonite communities did on a much larger scale where there were evangelistic meeting tents that held up to several thousand people. I noticed that youth joined my church at about my age. To join the church meant they became Christians and went to an "Instruction Class." Afterward, they were baptized and were then members of the church. I had been thinking about doing so as well.

One Sunday evening, I went to the revival service. The song leader rallied the congregation by leading us in singing "Power In The Blood" and "How Great Thou Art". If you have never heard a Mennonite congregation sing gospel songs in four part harmony, without accompaniment, you are missing a lot. It is very beautiful and melodic. After a prayer, there was the usual scripture reading. Then a male quartet sang "Jesus Paid It All" and another song I no longer remember.

This was followed by a special feature: a children's story. Mrs. Miller, the story lady that evening, had all the little kids from toddler age and up come up front and sit on the grass for a story. Two boys started pushing for the spot closest to the story teller. She told about Moses and how God saved his life when he was a baby. God saved his life because God wanted him to be a leader of Israel, she said. Something was sounding familiar. I started to squirm in my seat, feeling some heat. It reminded me of mom saying God saved my life in the car incident for some special purpose. Did mom put her up to this?

Mrs. Miller went on to say that If Jesus calls you to be a Christian, it is important that you not keep him waiting and that you "answer the door when he knocks." I knew I did not want to keep Jesus waiting. She went on and on about not disappointing Jesus until a cute little blond haired boy about four years old raised his hand. Mrs. Miller said, "yes Jerry, do you have a question?" No, he said, " But Jesus might get really, really mad waiting on you!" Every one laughed, Mrs. Miller patted the boy on the head and sent the children back to their parents. Another episode of "let's make the grown ups laugh" ended joyfully.

Now it was personal testimony time. The leader asked if anyone wanted to give a personal testimony. And yes, Brother Yoder stood up and wanted to thank God for saving his life when he got his arm caught in the corn picker. Praise the Lord! And then Sister Shank stood up, as a hush came over the crowd. Most everyone there had heard about her situation. She haltingly told of having "backslidden and fallen into sin" by getting involved with a married man. But the Holy Spirit spoke to her and she was now repenting of her sin and was recommitting her life to Christ. (I wasn't so sure it was the Holy Spirit that spoke to her. I had overheard mom tell her sister on the phone that the affair ended when the married man's wife found out and confronted her.)

But there was a soft murmur of "praise the Lords and Amens" through the tent. There was time for one more testimony….yes….Brother Sommers was thankful for the rain this afternoon. Now his crops could survive the dry spell this year. I too was thankful for the rain, because dad said if we did not get rain soon, we might lose most of our corn crop.

After testimonies, it was time for the offering. We were reminded that it was "more blessed to give than to receive" and large paper cups were sent down each isle to collect the money "for the work of the Lord." Now it was time for the sermon. Rev. Kaufman was an area Mennonite minister that had a weekly Christian radio program that was well liked in our area.

Rev. Kaufman told the Bible story of the small and despised tax collector,

Zacchaeus. Jesus loved him even though he was a sinner and was disliked by his society. Short Zacchaeus climbed a tree so he could watch from a distance. I always liked the Zacchaeus story because I felt like he did, on the outside looking in, and rejected by peers. Then Reverend Kaufman explained the plan of salvation of how Christ "shed his precious blood for our sins."

At the end of his sermon, Rev. Kaufman stressed how Jesus was waiting for us to accept him as our Savior so we would be "born again." He also used the metaphor of Jesus knocking on the door of our hearts waiting for us. He also said that the result of not accepting Christ might be we would die without Christ and be lost for eternity which meant being in hell described as a lake of fire. I guess that little boy who blurted out "Jesus might be mad" during the Children's Story time had it right after all.

While heads were bowed and eyes were closed and everyone softly sang verses of the hymn "Just As I Am," he asked for those who wanted to accept Christ to raise their hand. I raised my hand on the first verse, along with some other youth my age. The minister acknowledged each raised hand with "I see that hand, God bless you brother."

But then the minister lingered. After three verses of the song, he said there would be one more verse, "your last chance….don't leave here tonight without knowing you are saved, you might die in a car accident on the way home tonight and be lost." An insurance salesman once told me that this technique was called "backing up the hearse to the client's front door." He said it was very effective in closing the sale when selling Life Insurance.

Indeed it was. Might you know, during verse four there was another hand raised and so the minister had us sing another verse when he promised "this was the last one" for the third time.

The service was already going on one hundred minutes. I had to pee badly but refused to embarrass myself by leaving during the altar call. I began to work against the minister by praying, "please no more during this verse, don't encourage that preacher or we will never get out of here."

Wrong, there was another repentant sinner during verse five. How long could this go on, I wondered. Finally, it ended after verse six. I made a bee-line, or I could say "pee-line" for the bathroom. Oh yes! What a relief. I made it!

After relief, I met individually with a counselor who asked if I wanted to be a Christian. I said "yes," and he led me to a private room and talked to me to see if I understood what I was doing. He then led me in a short prayer of asking forgiveness for my sins and asking Christ into my heart.

I felt very relieved of the guilt and shame I had been carrying for being such a bad boy in my family.

I, along with other youth, attended 10 weeks of a required "Instruction Class." It was a kind of Mennonite catechism in preparation for baptism and church membership. Of course, I always had my booklet filled out and knew every answer. Some of the other boys forgot their booklets or missed classes. Tsk! Tsk!

When the time came for baptism, six of us boys lined up at the front of our local Mennonite church to be baptized. We had all accepted Christ and had finished our Instruction Class, a catechism of Mennonite beliefs. Baptism was a solemn occasion where we made public our vows to live as Christians according to the beliefs of the church.

The six of us were facing the altar on our knees on the hardwood floor at the front of the church. Rev. Miller, the younger minister held a pitcher of water and was to pour some holy water into the cupped hands of Bishop Yoder who was to then release it on the head of the new member, with some incantations. Bishop Yoder must have been in his 80's and had the shakes.

Rev. Miller evidently poured way too much water into the bishop's hands so when Bishop Yoder released it on Larry, the first candidate, it flowed off his head and on the hardwood floor—making a "peeing" noise. No big deal, except that some of the boys started snickering and squawking as they tried not to laugh audibly.

Of course, the more you try to squelch a laugh, the worse it is. Bishop Yoder paid no attention and went on to Alvin, the second candidate. The boys were muffling their snickers fairly well. Me, St. James, was doing excellent at keeping my pious composure, that is until one of the boys farted and the whole row of us giggled audibly! Even I squeaked a giggle between my clenched teeth. I was so embarrassed for us all! C'mon guys, shut up! This is serious! How could these boys really be Christians if they laughed at their baptism, I judged. Tsk! Tsk!

Here in this most sacred of ceremonies, where we were joining with the saints in the holy and pure church of Christ and were to be putting away all earthly desires and sins of the flesh, at this moment, these bad boys laughed at water dripping on the floor! My ego had a field-day feeling superior. Even then I knew my 'holier than thou" attitude was a sham and I did not feel right in being judgmental of others.

Today, as I read the Gospels, I feel quite sure if Jesus of Nazareth had been present at the baptism in person that winter evening, he would have belly laughed with the boys and told judging James "Go and get a life!"

I was eager to attend church meetings and usually did not need to be pressured to go. At church there was positive attention from adults. I was seen as more "religious" than my peers and for a young boy seeking approval, that was a good thing.

While becoming a Christian and being baptized was helpful in some ways there was a downside to it. Now that I was a "Christian", I was expected to act like one and that meant to be pure, chaste and loving in my day to day life. That would include not getting angry, not pleasuring myself and certainly not fighting with siblings. That lasted about a day and a half, as I recall.

A few Mennonite preachers preached a doctrine of "Eternal Security" which meant that once you were saved, you would be assured of heaven even if you sinned again. But the majority opinion was that this was wrong. You could not count on heaven if you slid back into sin, other wise known as "backsliding." So trying to be a good Christian was a part of my daily struggle.

By that time in my life, Mrs. Fry, my overweight fourth grade teacher, told us about the threat of nuclear war with Russia. I saw pictures in our *Weekly Reader* of Nikita Khrushchev and his ranting about how "we will bury you." It also showed the Russian nuclear bombs stacked on a pile. We were told that there was one of those for every major U.S. city. I looked closely to see if "Cleveland" was written on any of them. I understood they could drop one of those bombs on us at any time without notice. We practiced a bomb drill by getting under our seats at school, just in case.

I was scared. If the Russians dropped a bomb on us before I repented of my sins, I might go directly to hell. It all seems like such a trite and childish game now. But to a sensitive young boy like me, it was cause for worry. There were many quick prayers of confession, like when a jet broke the sound barrier overhead. I would pray "Oh God, don't let the Russians bomb us before"…... and then I would insert an event like getting home that night or the 8th grade class party. After all, it took all the guts I had to call Ruth Ann, the smart girl with the wiggly pony tail, and ask her to go with me to the party. She said yes. I would bargain with God to be good if he would only oblige my wishes.

Even with all my worries, my pubescent hormones started kicking in and I was horny much of the time. I rode the public school bus for my first three years of high school. I usually sat on the school bus about three fourths of the way back, positioned so I could hear some of the "dirty jokes" (hetero of course) whispered by the bad boys in the back of the bus. I was aroused by hearing sex talk and "dirty words." Every few minutes there was a burst of laughter from the boys back there as another dirty joke punch-line cracked them up. I tried very hard to keep a straight face. I was close enough to hear the jokes but far enough away I could pretend not to hear. I was aroused by the dirty words they used. And they taught me "Swearing 101," all part of a good public school education.

Yet, I was conflicted. After all, I had an image to maintain. Oh how I wanted to be part of the boys at the back of the bus, but the dominant part of me felt compelled to present the St. James image to the world. What a burden. The truth was I felt different from the other boys and was not in their group. My judgmental attitude toward them made any acceptance impossible.

In a Mennonite church youth paper in 1966, I was referred to as "St. James" when it reported on a weekend youth retreat I helped to lead at one of our church's camps. Of course this was tongue in cheek since Mennonites do not recognize special saints. Even so, it was quite heady to be so highly regarded at age 22.

At age fourteen I started high school and so was allowed to be part of our church youth group. There I found a social group and some acceptance and approval. I sometimes talked with our youth minister who seemed more understanding of youth. I wanted to impress him and others at our church and was quite successful in doing so.

Our national youth organization was promoting Bible memory and quizzing at the time I entered the youth group. Since I had a sharp mind I could memorize scripture quite easily and recall things. Over several years I memorized the entire books of Philippians and First John word for word from the King James Version of the Bible. I also memorized parts of the book of Romans and some of the Psalms. I did enjoy learning these verses, not only for the competitive quizzing but also for my own personal and spiritual nourishment. I can still recite some of these verses today. I particularly loved the Psalms that spoke of God showing himself through nature because that was my closest personal experience of God's presence.

Being part of the youth group and eventually providing leadership for the group was very helpful. It helped me feel accepted and positive about the gifts I had for organization and creative programming. I got lots of strokes from other youth and my family who seemed proud of what I was doing. I sometimes befriended other lonely youth I met in the public school and community. I certainly knew what it felt like to be lonely and "not belong". One of these young people I befriended and his family joined our local church. This brought me praise from my family and church.

I was frustrated, though, with our local church. I noticed that God seemed to change his mind every year or two. What was sin one year was no longer a sin a few years later. So which way is it, I wondered, does He or doesn't He want us Christians to look different from the world? And is it OK to have a TV or isn't it? And if so, what size can it be? I noticed that God supposedly had the same opinion as the local minister of our church and it varied from congregation to congregation. So much for revelation.

Either God was totally capricious or we humans were projecting all kinds of meanings and understanding into the sky and by saying "God says, or scripture says." I began to devalue the opinion and interpretations of all ministers and not take them very seriously because of that. And clearly, one could prove almost anything one wanted to from the Bible by assembling certain verses together. I learned to distrust anyone who was too certain that they had THE truth. It was those individuals who were the most cruel and judging.

It seemed that most of the Mennonite folk in my church wanted to be accepted in society. Some were confused why we were sometimes pointed out and snickered at in public.

Aunt Cora was a moderately obese lady in our church who wore long plain dresses and black stockings. Her dresses had a cape, a second layer of cloth over the front so the shape of the breasts was obfuscated. Her long hair was usually rolled up on her head in a tight bun and topped off with the white mesh prayer bonnet that covered her hair completely. We Mennonite boys jokingly referred to this prayer covering as a "milk strainer," because it looked like the round white strainer discs dairy farmers used when pouring milk into 10 gallon cans.

Aunt Cora had a reputation of being a great cook. I was excited when mom said she invited our family over for dinner Sunday after church. Having dinner together with friends like this was really part of our religion. Our family frequently had friends or relatives over for meals. Yes, the get-togethers were about good comfort foods but it was much more about sharing stories and finding out the "goings on" of others. It was a way to stay connected with each other in our close community.

For four days I was looking forward to a great meal at Aunt Cora's and was not disappointed. I loved to eat homemade cooking and could do so without any worry about cholesterol or fat content. Aunt Cora was quite a talker. She stuttered, had a strong Pennsylvania Dutch accent and spoke with a lisp. Any two of those would have been entertaining enough but all three together made listening to her quite fun. And if that weren't enough, she spoke so fast, or tried to, she would gasp for breaths part way through a sentence. I loved hearing her talk because she was so expressive and dramatic.

Aunt Cora presented a wonderful meal of fried chicken, baked ham, spinach garden salad, mashed potatoes, corn, and a choice of banana cream or pecan pie. I was not much into salads those days but I loved her fresh spinach salad with sweetened miracle whip and vinegar dressing, diced scallions and crumbled bacon bits tossed in.

Once everyone was stuffed, the men retired to the living room to talk of machinery and crops. At least I supposed that's what they talked about. I don't know for sure because I stayed in the kitchen, sitting at the table, listening to Aunt Cora's stories as she and my mother washed and dried the dishes.

Cora said to my mother, "Say Elsie, ya shoulda seen vot appened to my sister Effie and me yesterday. I vas so upset, I chust can't get over it! Couldn't sleep last night barely a wink tinkin about it."

My mother, who spoke in clear and proper English, said, "Why, Cora, what happened that upset you so much?"

"Vel," Cora said, "Vee ver in that high-falutin (meaning expensive) fabric store in Wooster, lookin fer yard goods to make me a new dress. I chust never haff enuff. Vel I vas in vun of the isles lookin at all da perty fabric and ven I turned the corner, I saw the two youngin girls at the check out counter pointin an making schput (a German phrase meaning mocking) of us. They ver laughin so any vun could hear."

"Oh no," mother said as she dried another dish, "those girls should not be doing that, it was so rude of them. What's wrong with them anyhow?"

"Ya, vell," Cora continued, "I know they shouldn't hav but they chust kept laughin and pointin, effen after they saw us watchin' em."

'I probably would have left the store if they did that to me", mother said.

"Vell, I vood haff but ve found this lovely material for my dress and ve chust bought it quick and left. I vas so mad!"

"That's too bad Cora, no one deserves to be treated like that, shame on them!" mother said.

"Ya vell, I chust don't see vat effry vun tinks is so funny bout us Mennonites," Cora exclaimed, as she put another plate in the drainer rack.

I thought Aunt Cora was funny by the way she talked and dressed. But at the core I knew the kinds of feelings of being different that she had. While I looked like other children, I knew I was part of a religious sect that was at odds with the secular world and this bothered me greatly. Instead of noticing that what made us different from others, simply made us different, and leave it at that, there was the added egocentric belief, endorsed by God, that what made us different, also made us better than others. And the implication was that "we" had the true faith and other faiths were wrong. This invariably leads to pride and judging of others.   —

Chapter Six

Secret "Boyfriends"

One of the most powerful, controlling inhibitors of joy and freedom in our family and church was the tired old phrase I learned to hate so much… "What would people think?" What would people think if they saw you at that movie? What would the neighbors think if we bailed hay on Sunday afternoon before it rained? Or, What would the preacher think if we got a TV, or if my sister Barb cut her hair short?" That often seemed to be the bottom line in decision making.

The message I got about this is that we are to live our lives not from our own center of desire or belief, but rather from some external judging neighbor, preacher, church or family member who might be offended or think less of us. It is more important to conform to others expectations than to be honest and true to one's beliefs. In being taught a phony humility, we were also taught to distrust ourselves.

I set aside many of my intellectual doubts during these high school years because I was very active and busy with life. For some reason Aunt Ruby, the one who hired me to help my cousin Kaye Jean do housework and baking, tried to match me up with a girl my age that she admired. She arranged for us to meet and I actually did like the girl because she was very intelligent and pretty. I would daydream of having dates with her but also very nervous at the thought.

I had another girlfriend for most of my senior year of high school. She was my date for the Senior Moonlight and Roses Banquet at the end of the school year. We wrote funny love letters every few days during that next summer and had a few dates. I liked girls more as friends than girlfriends. I felt much closer and accepted by girls than the other guys because my interests and sense of humor was more like those of the girls I knew.

My desire to please others was so strong that it was no problem to conform to social expectations. The social pressure for dating and marriage was pervasive. I did want to be a father and raise a family because I liked children. I do not think I really ever wanted to be married heterosexually, but since marriage was the only legitimate way to have a family, I willingly conformed.

My first year of college was at a small Mennonite college in Kansas. My roommate Dan was tall and thin. I had a crush on him but carefully hid it so he would not find out he was rooming with a homo. Dan had a beautiful blond girlfriend and talked about what they did or wanted to do on their dates. He probably thought I was really listening to him as he talked. But my mind was more on Dan. Sometimes Dan and I would wrestle and horseplay on his bed or mine, all in good fun and teasing. But boundaries were fairly clear—touching each other below the waist was a no-no.

One night in the spring of the year, Dan and I had both completed our studies for the evening and were in our briefs. The lights were out. We were talking about school work and dating like we often did, in our separate beds. School would be out soon and we would be going our separate ways. I so much wanted to tell him what I was feeling about him but I was sure he did not feel the same way. I was his good friend, and that was it. I struggled not to say anything explicit or reveal my feelings about him. It seemed, at least for me, I talked about everything that was nothing and nothing that was everything.

I hinted in a general way about feelings for guys. Dan was very intelligent and most likely knew what was going on but we were both in denial. Dan wanted to talk about his love feelings for his girlfriend. I talked a little about my girlfriend as that was expected, but in a detached way. Oh, yes I did have a few dates that year and several with the same girl but I soon lost interest in her.

After Dan went to sleep that night, I quietly left the room and went down to the quiet prayer room and locked the door. Tearfully, I pled, "Please God, take these feelings away! Why do I feel the way I do? Why me? Where are you God? Are you really there?" Silence. No answers. I wondered—if God were all-powerful, why couldn't he take these feelings of attraction to men away? Eventually I went back to bed and to sleep as I had classes the next day.

My college years two through four were at Malone College in Canton, Ohio. I transferred there so I could save money by staying at home. Malone was a twenty-seven and a half minute commute from my home, if the roads were clear. I had it timed to arrive just in time for class. Malone College, now Malone University, is a school operated by the Society of Friends (Quakers) in Ohio. I worked construction for my uncle to help pay tuition and saved money by staying at home.

I loved learning about history, earth science, political science, sociology, economics and, of course, psychology. Increasingly, I started thinking more independently and learned to ask critical questions about the larger world.

As I learned more in school, I observed that the timeline held forth by literal interpreters of the Bible was totally erroneous. I learned that scientists discovered that our world was not millions but rather *billions* of years old and that we as humans, in some form, have been here for at least three or four million years.

A class I took in Theories of Counseling taught by Dr. Barrett, a psychology professor, stirred my interest in psychology and counseling. He had a ruddy complexion, blond hair, moustache and a short skuzzy beard. He had a good sense of humor and his gentle smile and soft eyes made him approachable. In the class, Dr. Barrett taught us about the work of Carl Rogers who developed "Client-Centered Therapy". He explained the value of having "unconditional positive regard" for those we try to help. This impressed me.

I talked with Dr. Barrett one time in his office at the college about my interest in a career in psychology and counseling. He listened very carefully and openly to what I said. This felt loving. After years of feeling the pain of being misunderstood and talked at or preached at, this was a breath of fresh air!

I had never been listened to like that before. To be heard on my own terms without being judged was exhilarating. It opened my eyes to a new way of relating to people that seemed genuine and loving. I knew then that I wanted to learn more about counseling and psychology so I could be more loving in my relationships with people.

Here was another defining moment in my life. I decided I wanted to spend my life listening to people and helping them love and accept themselves as they are. While being fully aware of the evil things we humans do to each other, I affirmed the inner goodness that is there as well. After twenty–five years of my private practice in counseling psychology, I am still living out that commitment I made my senior year of college.

Because Dr. Barrett was such an empathetic listener, it was easy to understand why he had such a thriving psychotherapy practice in Canton. After becoming licensed as a psychologist in Ohio, I worked in Dr. Barrett's private practice office for several years. I was honored when he asked me to teach several of his psychology classes at Malone College one summer while he was on sabbatical. I loved teaching but was disappointed in the "how many pages does this paper have to be and can it be double spaced" attitude of some of the students who wanted to do only the bare minimum to squeak by.

In my senior year at Malone College, I had a schedule conflict and needed an Adolescent Psychology class credit for my major in order to graduate with my class. I was able to take that class at Walsh College, a Catholic college about three miles from Malone. I was very excited to hear about adolescent sexual development and experimentation. Of course, the Catholic Brother teaching the class only alluded to same-sex experimentation as "a phase" some boys go through during adolescence.

While taking that class, I met another student in the class named Paul. He had a preppy look with hazel eyes, curly blond hair and muscular arms. He had a broad, friendly smile and great sense of humor.

One day after class he introduced himself to me and suggested we have lunch together after one of the classes. I saw no harm in making a new friend, even if he was Catholic!

Since Paul stayed in the dorm at Walsh and did not have a car on campus, I drove us to McDonald's that first lunch. He told me he was from a large Catholic family from Massachusetts and was majoring in psychology. That sparked my interest. Like me, he was in his senior year and would soon graduate. I told him I was raised Mennonite, but somehow he seemed to already know that. He said he was curious about my Mennonite upbringing.

I understand you are not allowed to go to dances, he said.

"Well, it is looked down upon but some of our young people go anyway. I think its ok to dance," I said.

"Are you allowed to go to movies?" he asked.

"That's quite common nowadays with our young people, and I do go to some movies," I replied.

"But don't your people wear those black hats and have beards, he asked. "No, you are thinking of the Amish, similar to Mennonites but different. The Amish are much more strict and conservative in most ways," I explained.

We talked about our class discussions about adolescents, and how more youth are becoming sexually active earlier. Then Paul said,

"Well, I'm sure you don't believe in sex before marriage."

I was taken aback by his directness. "That is definitely against our church's teaching. But I don't necessarily agree with that teaching or many of my church's teachings," I said.

Paul smiled mischievously, and winked. I returned the smile nervously. He could tell I was becoming uncomfortable.

We then chatted more about our school programs and the class we were taking together. I liked Paul right from the start. It was unusual though for a guy I never knew before to reach out to me in friendship. I was puzzled, uneasy, suspicious and interested. What did Paul really want, I wondered? I longed to have male friends, not just classmates or superficial contacts with guys at church so I allowed the friendship for a brief time.

One beautiful spring day after our lunch, as I pulled in the driveway by his dorm, I stopped the car to chat a little longer. We only had a few more weeks left in the class and would not likely see each other again. Paul said he had enjoyed getting to know me. I nodded likewise.

Then Paul gently reached his hand over the console gear shift of my car and lightly touched my thigh. I was aroused and was enjoying the attention. I touched his hand and held it in mine for a few minutes, rubbing it gently. We looked in each other's eyes furtively, saying nothing. It felt so good. Too good. I started to become afraid and I moved his hand back to his lap. I could tell he also was aroused. Paul looked at me and said, "Would you like to see my room?" I looked away because I knew this was not about a room visit.

I felt excited and scared. I froze. His invitation, which really wasn't very subtle, still caught me off guard. Later I could see the signs of his interest in me were there all along. In a moment I had to decide. Would I listen to my body this time and explore this friendship and sensuality? Or hide again as I had always done before.

Of course I would like to see his room, and him too! I was clearly aware of my interest in Paul but at that time I was too frightened by my own natural desires to allow myself to explore them with anyone, especially someone who liked me and whom I liked.

I grasped Paul's hand again and said in a quivering voice, "Uh, I….uh… right now, I better get home to study for our exam on Friday." He looked away. I could see the disappointment in his face. He knew it was an excuse as did I. He said, "Ok, maybe another time." Yes. Maybe. I was trembling as I drove home that day. I came so close to something real, something honest, and something powerful and left it slip away. I was not ready.

I had a part-time job cleaning a small barn for a rich man who owned Arabian horses. The farm was on my way home so I stopped to do my chores. I went through my routine work there but my mind was mulling over what had just happened. I was relieved with my decision, but also regretted it. My fear killed my joy. I was not prepared to let myself experience what my body was wanting and needing for many years and what I remembered from childhood experiences. I was so close and yet so far.

I only saw Paul a few times afterward in that class and glanced at him wistfully with a tear in my eye. He smiled back as if he understood. I wonder how my life might have been different had I accepted his invitation to visit his room. I most likely would have gotten married anyway. One time I saw a sign that said, "My karma ran over my dogma." Well, eventually it did, but not on that day.

I now believe that on one level the drama about my vocation and my religious beliefs was about establishing my independence, claiming my right for self determination and maintaining intellectual honesty.

But at an even deeper level, my vocational and religious rebellion was really about my unacceptable sexual impulses, feelings and desires. I felt certain I could never really be myself if in a church leadership role. St. James' hope for me was fading fast; his halo was becoming more tarnished over time.

Those pesky sexual feelings kept coming up over and over. And the more I pushed them back the stronger they became. I refused to trust the wisdom of my own body. Instead my arrogant and all-controlling ego wanted to have its way and force me into its ideal shape that it thought would please God and others and would get recognition.

The issues of vocation and intellectual doubts I raised actually served as a smoke screen for that which was hidden and repressed inside. If only I had realized that at age fourteen instead of forty four! But I have absolutely no regrets. Who am I to question the wisdom of my life journey? It was unfolding just as it was to be, whether I knew it or not.

Chapter Seven

Doubts

In 1967, I met my Carolyn while teaching social studies at Rockway Mennonite High School, a church-sponsored school in Kitchener, Ontario. She is from Johnstown, Pennsylvania. She was very lovely with soft petite hands and gentle ways. She was the home economics teacher at the Rockway school and the students loved and respected her.

Carolyn is an intelligent, open minded, and incredibly nurturing woman. I found her refreshingly feminine and sensitive. She allowed me the freedom to be myself as our relationship grew. Even though her family was quite conservative Mennonite, Carolyn was open to new ideas and accepted people as they were without judging.

Carolyn graduated from the liberal "Goshen College" in Indiana, where Mennonite girls cut their hair, wore tight jeans, went to movies and seldom wore the white prayer veiling. Carolyn and I became close friends quickly and the romantic attraction grew during my second year of teaching at the school. In many ways, we were perfect for each other. My heart responded enthusiastically to her loving acceptance and affirmation.

I was relieved to find that I did have interest in and could be aroused by the opposite sex. I felt love for Carolyn because she was easy to love and was physically attractive. We enjoyed going to movies and music concerts together. This seemed to be the perfect solution to my "problem" of same sex feelings.

43

I could marry, be accepted in my family, the church and society and raise a family like other men my age. And since I was sexually responsive to her, I thought perhaps my same sex feelings would just go away. And besides, I really wasn't gay after all, was I? How could I be gay? I was a born again Christian and a Mennonite and so it seemed impossible that I was gay. I never met a gay Mennonite until I met Keith many years later.

Carolyn and I became engaged in February of 1969 and married that August. We were apart from each other the summer before we married because we had summer jobs in two different places. But we kept in touch with almost daily letters and some phone calls. It seemed I had an urgency to get married but also some apprehension. I remember the relief on my mother's face when I told her I was engaged. She had been worrying about me. She did not say exactly why and I didn't ask. Could it be that she wondered if I was gay?

The day before the wedding, Carolyn and I were driving back to her parent's home in her Ford Falcon after picking up our marriage license at the Somerset County Courthouse. I wanted and needed to say something to Carolyn but was very afraid. The tension was building inside me.

Finally, I stammered, "Carolyn, uh, I'm concerned about something—I'm not sure what I feel". She said, "What is it?"

I said, "I just don't feel for you like I think a man should feel for his fiancé the day before he is getting married."

"What do you mean?" she asked cautiously.

"I don't know what it is. I guess I am a little uneasy with getting married. I love you but I am not sure I feel like I should feel the day before getting married. It's something inside. I suppose most guys are nervous the day before their wedding but it seems more than that."

"But Jim," she said, "I am sure that you love me—I can see it in so many ways— and I love you. I think it will be ok." I was reassured. That was the end of the conversation. After all, it was obviously too late to cancel a wedding that was the next day.

Later that evening, I was talking alone with John, a close friend whom I had asked to be in my wedding. He said, "Jim, I am concerned. Maybe you should reconsider getting married". I was stunned and completely caught off guard. "What do you mean by that? " I asked.

" Ahhh, what do you think about the other kind of sex?" he said.

"You mean like sex before marriage?" I asked.

"No, remember when we slept together on the many trips we made for the youth work we did?" I nodded yes. "When we were in the same bed you put your leg against me and were aroused. I had to push you off of me!"

I was shocked to learn this because John had never told me about this before. Interestingly, I honestly did not recall those times but believed John was telling the truth. He never would have said this if it had not been true. My heart was beating rapidly by now and my throat was becoming very dry. I started to become aroused by just talking about this with John.

"I—I—I thought about it but never have. I'm not sure what two guys do together, I stammered." That was a lie.

Well, I'm not sure either, he said. I'm not interested in guys that way. I enjoy girls. Let's just forget it, OK?"

I was relieved to just drop the subject. But then John added:

"You could still call the wedding off, you know. Don't go ahead with it if you aren't sure."

"No, I can't do that, its way too late. I love Carolyn and everything is going to be OK!" I said.

"Well, I hope so" he said as the conversation ended.

How could I even discuss this issue with John on the eve of my wedding? No way could I "reconsider" at this late date. Brothers, sisters, aunts and uncles either had already arrived in Johnstown, Pa, or were on the way. Tomorrow was to be the happiest day of my life. *Right.*

What was happening to me—why all this on the day before my wedding—and why am I aroused now? So many questions. I felt confused and troubled. Just when I thought my problem was being resolved, it wasn't. Those feelings had to be repressed and were.

I had difficulty getting to sleep that night as I was thinking about the conversation in the car with Carolyn and then John that evening. I eventually feel asleep from the exhaustion of a busy day. The next day the wedding ceremony and reception proceeded as planned.

I did not have contact with John for thirty nine years. Last year I found his address through an internet search. Thirty nine years after he was in my wedding, I arranged a meeting with John and his wife in California when I was near his community on vacation. It was a very unusual reunion in that I knew John but in many ways did not know him now these many years later.

Both of us had changed. Interestingly, he chose to become a mental health professional as well and has had a stellar career in psychiatry.

After a short two day honeymoon, Carolyn and I pulled a U-Haul behind her 1967 baby blue Ford Falcon and drove to Richmond, Indiana. There we moved our few belongings into an apartment in the married student housing on the campus of Earlham College. I enrolled in a two year Master of Arts in Religion program at the Earlham School of Religion, a graduate school program of the college. My purpose was to learn about Christianity as well as other world religions in a setting that was open minded and academically rigorous.

Until this time, I only had a Sunday school understanding of Christianity and that did not satisfy my intellectual curiosity nor did many of those beliefs seem to have authenticity. If I was to find faith as an adult, I needed to have more depth of understanding and to choose after having learned and looked at alternative religious systems and beliefs. I was searching for a meaning to life and some truth I could know from within, an intrinsic faith. I had an open mind but not an empty mind as I started my classes. I did have some core values and beliefs that I brought to my searching but was genuinely open.

Within several months of starting school at E.S.R. in the fall of 1969, I had a significant dream. In my dream I was about twelve years old and was in the kitchen of our farm home on Swallen Road. Mother was standing by the sink looking out the kitchen window. I noticed that our house was burning down and was alarmed. The house was not in flames but all around the wood structure was smoldering and crumbling and slowly falling down.

In the dream I asked mother if someone had called the fire department. She said, "yes, your brother went over to the neighbors and they were supposed to call the Louisville Fire Department. But, that was a half hour ago." The fire trucks had not arrived yet and in my dream I recall thinking, "The fire trucks are never going to come, are they?"

In a panic, I ran upstairs to my bedroom and began sorting through my belongings and had to decide quickly what I would take and what I would leave behind. I put my diary and some pictures and the bronze medal I got from the American Legion in a box and ran out of the house into the back yard to safety. Then I awakened.

Some dreams, like this one, hardly need any interpretation. This dream represented exactly what I was going through in my life at that time. I had to decide, and with some urgency, what was of value from my home and church life and what I would leave behind. What I took was that which was irreplaceable — the record of my life journey, memories of the important people in my life and my self-esteem.

I was challenged by my studies at E.S.R. and loved what I was learning. Most of the classes required intense study which was good discipline for me.

My favorite professor was Dr. William Rogers, Ph.D., a psychologist and a theologian. He taught classes in theology and psychology. He also taught one on integrating the teachings of Freud, Adler and Jung with theological perspectives of Paul Tillich, Reinhold Niebuhr and Rollo May. I loved those classes and did well in them. I also looked up to Dr. Rogers as a mentor and role model. He had many of the qualities of my college professor Dr. Barrett. Dr. Rogers became my advisor and worked with me on my Master's Project. I spoke very highly of him in letters home. My mom wrote one letter expressing concern about what I was learning at this school.

Mom was well read and rightly proud of her high school education, which in her day was like a college degree is today. She particularly loved English and would sometimes quote phrases from Shakespeare or American poets. My love of learning was inspired by mom. She always encouraged her children to get a college and even graduate degrees.

Mom was uneasy about my going to what she considered to be a "liberal school." She was being influenced and frightened by one Oliver B. Greene, a conservative radio evangelist who warned of the dangers of liberal theology. She listened to him weekly as he incited fear in her about liberals in the church. He focused on the *absolute necessity* of believing in two doctrines: the literal virgin birth and the necessity of the blood of Christ for salvation.

At Easter time 1970, I was completing my first year of seminary. Carolyn and I were home for spring break. I was sitting on the large brown Lazy Boy chair in the living room of the new home my parents had built ten years earlier after selling the farm on Swallen Road. Mother was sitting in her favorite high back chair across from me.

"James", mom began, "I am concerned about what you are learning in seminary. I am afraid it is too liberal and not the right doctrine."

"What do you mean mom?" I said cautiously, sensing trouble.

"Do you believe in the virgin birth?" she queried.

"No mom, I do not believe that literally. I believe the writers of that part of the Bible were trying to show that Jesus was from God in a special way and were trying to promote Christianity. Other religions in that time also claimed special birth circumstances for their deities including visiting kings, astrological signs and miracles." I explained.

"Well James, that is exactly what I have been worrying about," mom said. "I am afraid this liberal theology you are getting at Earlham is leading you astray. You are getting away from Bible teachings."

"Do you believe the blood of Christ had to be shed for our salvation?" mother inquired further.

"No mom, I do not believe that literally either," I said. "That theology is one way early Christians tried to fit the life of Jesus into the Jewish faith so it would be acceptable to Jewish people. I do not believe in an angry God who needs blood sacrifice to appease his anger and forgive sins," I explained. I had learned about other Christian theories of the atonement that made more sense to me but this was not the time to try to go into them.

Mom looked away, and became visibly agitated. She bit her lower lip and continued, "I was afraid when you went to that liberal school this would happen," she lamented. "I just wish you had gone to our church seminary."

I was angry and agitated as well. At twenty eight, mom was trying to tell me what I had to believe to be saved. "Mom, I would like you to trust me to find my own answers through my studies and prayer," I said.

Mother left the room visibly upset because of our disagreements. After she left the room, I remember starting to laugh to myself. I thought, "Did God really write down the two doctrines of the virgin birth and blood sacrifice on a piece of litmus test paper and UPSd them to this radio evangelist? I've read about the Dead Sea Scrolls but never heard of the Litmus Test Scrolls. And did God include directions in the package telling preacher Greene to judge every human being for heaven or hell based on whether they believed these two doctrines? How ridiculous and laughable."

I was chuckling to myself at those thoughts! And yet I was startled at how inappropriate laughter seemed given the intense argument I was having with mom. We were both in emotional pain and hurting and now I was laughing. What's wrong with this picture?

Actually, it wasn't funny. It fact I was very sad, and rather than cry I did the opposite to hide my pain and sadness. It took me a short time to let myself feel what was really there, my sadness, hurt and anger. And I felt wounded by mother's lack of trust in me now, when she always had been so proud of me before.

When mother came back in the room a half hour later I said, "Mother, I feel sad that we don't agree on these things and likely never will. We only upset each other by arguing and nothing changes. So, I don't ever want to talk about this again."

"Well, maybe it's best then if we don't," mom said, "but I can't sleep at night worrying about this."

"Mom," I said, "I am sorry this upsets you so much that you can't sleep but I am not going to lie to you and tell you what you want to hear just to please you. That would be dishonest, wrong and insulting to you. This is just the way it is so lets just agree to disagree!" And we never did talk about theology again.

My challenge was to accept my mom as she was with some compassion for whatever fears and loss she was experiencing by her star son going astray. Mom had already made huge changes in her beliefs over the years by accepting more liberal practices of her church and family. And, mother was absolutely sincere in her convictions. Her intentions were noble but it was difficult to recognize that when submerged in my emotional pain.

I have studied the life and teaching of Jesus of Nazareth as a child and in seminary as an adult. I confess there is a wisdom and authenticity there that has repeatedly and deeply inspired me. I resonate with his teachings about the error of self-righteousness and the wisdom of following the way of peace and justice among all peoples of the earth. The way he treated people respectfully and lovingly regardless of their life situation is incredible. His words and deeds as recorded in the Gospels and elsewhere continue to speak to my inner being in ways that other writings do not. His loving attitude stirs me to more genuine self-acceptance and acceptance of others as they are.

But affirming miracles and mysteries was always problematic for me. Bishop John Shelby Spong, in his book, *Jesus for the Non-Religious,* offers a radical and refreshingly honest understanding of Jesus. He maintains that

"…we need not pretend to believe the supernaturally unbelievable in order to be Jesus disciples. We need only to see all that life can be – and in the ability of the human Jesus to open our eyes to this vision, a new sense of what it means to be divine begins to emerge."

I believe the life that was in Jesus is the life energy of the universe and in all living things. He showed us that we have this divine light within us. Jesus was fully, radically human and in his humanness he showed us what spirituality truly is. This demonstration will enrage the pious then and now.

I since have learned that the human ego invariably represses awareness of our Source as it struggles to find its own life apart from that Source. There is no need to label that repression as bad or sinful; that only complicates the problem and layers shame and guilt on a natural process. It is what it is. I know each one of us has the potential to act violently toward ourselves or our fellow man and it has caused tremendous suffering and pain. I don't think it helps to attribute that evil to a devil or Satan. Fear will motivate us humans only a short time and needs constant reinforcing to work. The results it produces are temporary and superficial. What it typically brings is more trying and self-effort to not only be good enough but to be perfect.

During the two years at Earlham, I was also adjusting to married life. It was stressful, as I was in school full time and Carolyn was working full time for the County Health Department. There was a two mile path around the student housing area and a retreat center. We went for many walks and talks. On some of the walks we tried to process our feelings about our relationship and be supportive of each other.

As might be expected given my same-sex attraction and conflicted feelings, I soon was unhappy in my marriage. I was wanting and needing sexual intimacy very frequently. In part, I was just married, young and horny. But for me there was more to it. I think I was also acting out my insecurity about my sexual orientation. I was trying to prove to myself I was a normal heterosexual man.

For a period of time, I blamed Carolyn for our differences, which was very unfair to her. But no matter how many long-walk discussions we had, not much changed. Only later did I admit that most of our marital problems were really unresolved feelings within myself about my attraction to men. When I could acknowledge that to myself, our relationship was more honest and not as conflicted.

I was told by a psychology teacher-counselor in my freshman year of college that these feelings for men would likely go away after marriage. I wanted to believe that so much I left his office with hope, but it was false hope. He was ignorant about homosexuality and wrong. The same sex feelings were less intense for the first few years of our marriage but they never went away. Instead of listening to my truth inside, I trusted his words.

In the second year of graduate school at Earlham, I worked up the courage to have a private counseling session with my mentor, Dr. Rogers. I did not sleep well the night before our appointment. I knew that if he was to be of any help, I had to be completely honest with him. I confided to him my feelings about my marriage but also my same sex attraction since a young boy. I had almost given up hope of anyone really listening to me with understanding and without judging. But he did and that felt so damn good. It reinforced my desire to love people by listening to them.

Dr. Rogers asked a few good questions about my experiences growing up. He also reflected what I said so I could listen to myself. What a relief! Thankfully, he did not offer any easy reassurance that my marital problems would work out in time. I could sense that Dr. Rogers understood the conundrum I would have to deal with eventually. He knew and accepted that there was no easy answer or quick fix and had the wisdom not to offer any.

I left his office discouraged and somewhat depressed because there was no ready solution. But also relieved. While I was concerned about these feelings of attraction to men, his listening and reflection helped me acknowledge them to myself as real and not contrived. And most importantly, Dr. Rogers did not judge my same sex attraction as sinful, wrong or sick.

Chapter Eight

Nesting

After graduating from the Master of Arts Degree in Religion at E.S.R, Carolyn and I moved back to the London, Ontario area. In previous years, I had led a successful summertime coffee house program in Ontario in a summer resort town. We moved back to Ontario because a group of Mennonite businessmen in the area were starting a youth activities center and hired me to manage it. I was also hired part time to plan and lead retreats for area churches.

During that first year in Ontario, Carolyn became pregnant with our daughter Jennifer Joy. I was very excited when Carolyn told me the news. Planning for our first child brought Carolyn and I much closer together as a couple. We were making a family together. We moved into a two-bedroom house trailer that had an additional family room built onto it.

I loved having a child and Jennifer was always a very special delight. I have a picture of me holding her on my lap at about six months old. My guitar is on my lap in front of her. I have long hair and a Mennonite "strip" beard running along my chin-line. I am playing my guitar and singing her a song, most likely the song I had written for her. "Jen-ni-fer, Jen-ni-fer, with love to us you came. Jen-ni-fer Jen-ni-fer Joy's your middle name!" Once she was two, we got a Jolly Jumper, which attached to a doorframe. Jennifer loved to jump up and down in that jumper for what seemed like hours at a time.

Jennifer spoiled my wife and me by sleeping through the night within a month after she was born. However, I was so absorbed with career advancement and making a living at that time, I think the miracle and wonder of birth did not fully register with me like it did when my grandson was born in 2007.

After several years in Ontario, my wife and daughter and I moved back to northeast Ohio. I was offered a counseling job in Akron working with nonviolent men who were furloughed early from prison to go to school or work.

My son Leif was born in May of 1974. Carolyn and I chose that name because we had met a young man by that name at the coffee house in Ontario several years earlier. We understood the name origin comes from the word "love." I was thrilled to have a son to complete our family. He was a special little boy and cute as could be. He was typically fun-loving and very sociable.

In 1979, I completed my Ph.D. at The University of Akron and started my private practice. It was an exciting time. I chuckle now as I recall how I relished the role of psychologist when I first started. It's embarrassing, but I evidently had a secret fantasy of being Dr. Freud. I smoked my pipe during the wintertime and stroked my beard, with the proper inflection of "Uh—hum" in response to clients concerns or issues. Fortunately, that fantasy was set aside very soon in my career and I learned to relax and be myself.

I chose a doctoral dissertation topic that was of great interest to me and several professors in the Department of Guidance and Special Education at The University of Akron.

My dissertation was a construct validation study on Elizabeth Kubler-Ross' stages of death and dying. The research question was to find out if people really did go through the stages of denial, anger, bargaining, depression and acceptance in coping with death as Kubler-Ross claimed in her book *Death and Dying*. To complete the study I interviewed 72 people with life threatening illnesses and had them complete several inventories. This study studied me. It moved me deeply as I had to confront my own natural fear of death and dying. I was also keenly aware that my parents were getting up there in years and would most likely die before too many more years passed.

I kept a special journal of my emotional responses and feelings after each interview. This journal shows how I was struggling to face my own finitude and that of my aging parents. I looked at my own defenses against fear of death including denial, repression and anger.

After an inspiring interview with a man who had survived cancer, I wrote a journal entry as follows:

"When I see the end and know in the depths of my being that I too shall one day die, that my own life as I know it now will cease to be, then all that really matters is the now. Fill each moment with love, care, beauty, honesty. The trivia of social custom, status and privilege all fade. Then I come to my self, my sense of who I am, my true me, without the illusions, without the veneer and I begin to build again on the real me. The moistness in my eyes tells me I am home again."

* * * * *

My siblings and parents usually got together for a holiday meal at Thanksgiving or Christmas. The Christmas dinner after I got my Ph.D. was at my sister Barb's place. We all gathered around the extended table for the traditional turkey, dressing and mashed potatoes. For dessert, Barb usually made several great pies and Aunt Corrine would bring the family favorite dessert, Date Pudding.

Now it was time to sip coffee, lean back on our chairs and reminisce or talk about current family situations. Then one of my siblings spoke up —"we better be careful what we say here, we have a doctor with us now! He might analyze us—hee hee."

All eyes turned to me! What could I say? "So I played along. "Yes, you're right, I could pink slip some of you guys into the crazy ward if you're not careful." That got a good laugh. Then Uncle Bob said "We ought to have Dr. Jim talk to that couple from church who are separated because they can't stop fighting with each other. How would you handle that, Jim?"

I thought, "ah, the trap is set. See if the newly minted doctor can spout forth wise answers about a complicated problem with only a smidgeon of information." It was nice to be so highly regarded now that I might be able to jump high buildings with a single bounce. Were they really proud of me or just uncomfortable or both?

The first time this happened I bit hard and tried to give a wise answer. Of course it sounded stupid and I knew it, and they probably did also but were too polite to laugh. Subsequent occasions, I knew better than to take that bait so I would make some inane comments that sidestepped everything. But the first time I really embarrassed myself.

I guess in my family socialization training, called Childhood 101, I missed the session where it was taught that one sibling was not allowed to rise above the others or she or he might be embarrassed at family dinners.

One of my brothers jumped into the conversation..."Well—we all know what B.S. is, (it's bull sh __ __,) well, M.S. means "more of the same" and Ph.D. means "piled higher and deeper!" We all laughed in agreement. "Thanks for helping me learn humility today," I thought. Actually there is some truth in the joke. I always said that to get a Ph.D., one has to jump through so many hoops; it's like being in a circus.

During those early years as a psychologist, I was very interested in sex therapy and the work of Masters and Johnson. I was looking for help for my conflicted sexual feelings under the guise of getting continuing education credits to keep my psychology license. It was not hard to do both at once. I got a flyer announcing a seminar in Chicago given by these pioneers in sex therapy.

My wife and I and our two small children traveled by car to Elkhart, Indiana, where they stayed with my sister and her family while I went on to the sex therapy seminar in Chicago.

After learning about premature ejaculation, the squeeze technique and vaginismus the first day, I was eager to get to the topic of the second day: homosexuality. Dr. Masters had claimed some success in converting homosexuals to heterosexuals. However, his data was never fully accepted by other staff or colleagues and recently has been shown to lack credibility.

However, in the morning of day two, Dr. Robert Kolodny, a top research associate of Masters and Johnson, reported on research he had done on homosexuality that was divergent from Dr. Masters. I was all ears! He reported that same sex attraction and behaviors were frequently found in many animal species as well as all major societies in the history of the world. His research led him to believe that same sex attraction was a universal and natural variation of sexual desire and was not inherently abnormal or perverse. Unfortunately, Dr. Masters was not of the same opinion at that time but he permitted Dr. Kolodny's research to be done and reported on at the conference.

According to Dr. Kolodny's research, what was harmful and often seen as the pathology of the homosexual, was the guilt and shame associated with homosexuality caused by cultural taboos and prejudice in many western societies. The way society and families reacted to homosexuals determined the harm to the individual. The prejudice against gays drove many gays to the extremes of flaunting sexuality and promiscuity or the opposite extreme of repression and self-loathing.

I couldn't quite believe what I was hearing. I was very excited but nervous to hear what he was reporting. It felt very good to have a highly respected researcher affirming this truth. I began to think of my desires and myself differently. For the first time I thought that maybe I was not perverted for being attracted to men. Just maybe same sex attraction was a normal variation of human sexuality. What a thought! Since my anxiety about being gay was significantly reduced by what I was hearing, I was not as judging of my feelings. I was more open to exploring what it would be like to be with a man sexually.

This was about the time when the American Psychological Association removed homosexuality from its listing of psychological disorders. This change was made after a number of scientific studies proved that same sex desire and behaviors were not in themselves psychologically harmful.

I was elated, almost high as I drove from the seminar in Chicago to Indiana to pick up my wife and children. This seminar was the first time that I truly admitted to myself that I was most likely gay. What I had denied and repressed for so long I could now *start* to accept as part of my identity as a man.

And yet you hear the hedging? "most likely". And "admitting" sounds like admitting guilt. Yet admitting that something is so is a first step toward acceptance.

However, the closer I got to Indiana and my wife and two children, the more my mood became somber and quiet. I knew what I was feeling was not compatible with the family life I had started. I also knew I would not do anything to break up my family at that time. The long ride from Indiana to Ohio was unusually quiet. I feel fairly certain that Carolyn knew something was bothering me. There was no way I could talk about it then. I knew my life situation would not permit me to really explore my feelings for men freely. I had a career to develop and a family to raise.

Chapter Nine

Getting To The Point

My wife and I were a part of a small group within our local Mennonite church. It was called a "house church" because we met in our homes. There were two other married couples in our group plus Art, a pediatric nursing student at The University of Akron. We all lived within several blocks of each other in the Firestone Park area of Akron. For five years our group met weekly in one of our homes for a meal, singing and sharing. We supported each other with our children, careers and living economically.

I was quite sure that Art was gay because he never talked about or dated any girls. He had very refined musical and artistic tastes. You know the stereotypes. Even then I had some "gaydar."

One warm Sunday afternoon, I asked to talk to Art. I went to the home where he was staying. We sat on either end of the big couch. I was fidgety so we chatted superficially for a bit about his school program, work and our church group. Then I said. "Art, I have been wanting to ask you something for some time now but have been reluctant to do so. My question is—are you gay?"

Art looked me in the eye and without any hesitation said, "Yes I am. I decided I would not disclose this to anyone voluntarily. But, I also decided that if anyone asked me directly, I would be honest."

I then said, "Well Art, I have something to tell you. I have been struggling with feelings of attraction to men for years and have had a few brief same sex experiences, but I don't want to break up my family." He was empathetic, particularly since he knew and loved my wife and kids and visited in our home many times.

After talking with Art that Sunday afternoon, I came home and knew I had to talk to Carolyn that evening. I fidgeted through dinner and was distracted by what I knew I needed to do. Once the kids were in bed, we sat on the couch to talk. I started by telling Carolyn what Art told me and she was very accepting of him being gay.

Then with tears in my eyes and tension in my voice, I said "And I need to tell you something." I hesitated and then said, "I too am attracted to men sexually and I think I might be gay like Art."

Carolyn was understandably concerned and said "Well how do you know this?" I told her about some of my same sex feelings and experiences as a boy, adolescent and young adult. She did not ask if I had experiences with men since we were married and I did not volunteer that information. Part of me desperately wanted to be more explicit with her that night but I was too afraid. I had not yet accepted what I had admitted. I ended the conversation by suggesting that we talk about this another time. But another time did not come until I made my full disclosure to Carolyn twelve years later.

Art decided he would come out to our small "house church" group and did so the next week when we met. He was matter of fact about his disclosure and it was evident that he was fairly comfortable with himself as a gay man. He was the first openly gay Mennonite man I had met, and I was very impressed that he seemed happy and at peace with who he was. He was affirmed and supported in our house church group without any reservation. Art started to bring his boyfriend to our group picnics and social events and they were warmly received as a couple.

The Mennonite Church, as a denomination, was and is today on record as believing that all same sex relationships are sinful, without exception. They also affirm that all sexual involvement outside of heterosexual marriage is sinful. However our particular congregation, Summit Mennonite in Norton, had many teachers and other professionals as members. Our congregation welcomed Art and was more liberal and open minded. Other Mennonite congregations in the large cities of our country are generally more open and inclusive of gays. Some of those congregations that welcome gays have been kicked out of their regional conference associations and their ministers have been defrocked.

Interestingly, Carolyn and I could agree that gays should be welcomed in our home and church life. We embraced diversity in others but could not embrace and face our own differences at that time. We had our own de facto "don't ask, don't tell" policy. It was convenient for me to keep very busy with school, family and church activities. In many ways we had an ideal marriage and family. We had good communication skills and taught marriage communication classes together.

I tried to make friends with some of the other men in my local congregation, but that just did not feel right to me. The few attempts I made were awkward. Again, I felt different because I was different. I was trying to be someone I wasn't and it failed. And it was good it did because it kept me searching for my authentic self.

At that time, men who wanted to have quick sex with other men could find certain rest rooms or highway rest areas where casual sex encounters were sometimes available. I felt very guilty after having casual sex with men. I did not feel guilt about the sexual experiences themselves because it was mutual and pleasurable. I felt guilt for sneaking and hiding what I was doing. I knew it violated my marriage vows and that weighed on me very heavily.

Even though I was careful, I worried about getting an STD. I got tested quite often to reassure myself that I was OK. Psychologically, the possibility of getting caught raises the excitement and attraction of these casual experiences…as in the "forbidden fruit" syndrome. This can start a process that leads to excitement addiction where the risk of getting caught is thrilling and energizing. But casual, nameless, faceless sex also makes sex a banal pleasure that divorces it from emotional intimacy and loving. It was unsatisfying.

At first I maintained that since I was still functioning heterosexually, I must be bisexual. But eventually as I became more honest with myself, I started to accept that my orientation was for men. At no time did I seek to be with other women intimately.

In the summer of 1984, my wife and family took a vacation to Provincetown, MA. on Cape Cod. I knew it was a gay Mecca and that was one of the reasons I wanted to visit Provincetown. I was feeling very troubled inside about my feelings for men. Soon after we arrived, I started thinking about taking some time alone and walk along the beach to be by myself. There was something I wanted to say.

One afternoon, my family and I went to Race Point Beach at the tip of Cape Cod. This was as good of a time as any. I told my family I was going for a long walk. I started out with my sandals on but soon left them by a piece of driftwood, hoping to find them on my return.

I walked along the edge of the water letting the wet sand squish between my toes. I loved to feel the water washing over my hot feet. I picked up smooth stones to skip across the water. The water was cold but so refreshing. I walked and walked far away down the beach. I felt a tension building up inside the further I went. I sensed I was going to yell or scream something I felt deeply but was unsure of. I had to be certain I was far enough away so no one could hear me.

When I felt I had gone far enough, I saw a log at water's edge. I sat down on it and let the water lap over my hot feet. In an anguished voice, I screamed out as loudly as I could "I AM GAY!" I screamed details of what exactly that meant in my life. In this moment, I admitted what I had known inside for years but was never able to say explicitly. It was the start of some acceptance of myself as a gay man.

I also had a sense I was screaming my truth out to God as well, daring him to strike me dead. I remember noticing in amused puzzlement that God did not. He did not strike me with lightening and no whale jumped out of the ocean to swallow me up (unlike the story of Jonah in the Bible who was swallowed by a whale because he disobeyed God). This theistic God I worshiped and feared as a child did not act to punish me. Not that I really expected Him to, or did I?

In a strange way I was relieved and felt affirmed by the universe and God. After the screaming, I laid down on the sand on my back at water's edge. I could hear the waves lapping against the shore. I tasted the salt water on my dry lips. The waves slowly came in and washed over my legs, and then my genitals and then my chest. The ocean was baptizing me. I thought, "I had better get up now so I don't drown." But I did not. I wanted the baptism of full immersion. The water was now up to my neck. I held my breath as another wave washed over me and took my tears and sweat with it into the great Atlantic ocean.

I slowly got up from the water. My legs were as shaky as Daisy's newborn calf I had seen as a child on the farm on Swallen Road. I stumbled to the log, sat down and bent over with my head between my knees for a few minutes. Something felt "done and over with." Perhaps it was my self deception. Truth was setting me free. I then stood up and leaned back with my arms outstretched, facing the sun. The tension and tightness were gone, I breathed freely. Another step had been taken by coming out to myself.

Ten years later I returned to Race Point Beach alone and went to this special part of the beach to celebrate and remember that day of cleansing and coming out to myself. I took along some symbols of my life: a dollar bill, a page from a book, a picture of my partner and a condom. I buried them in the sand. In a halting voice, I sang words to the Christian hymn, "Come Thou Fount Of Every Blessing."

* * * * *

Some years later, at age 44, I had another short but very vivid dream. The old farm home on Swallen Road was heated with a coal furnace. In front of the furnace was a stoker, which was a metal bin for coal with an electric auger at the bottom. When the thermostat said heat was needed the stoker auger would bring crushed coal into the furnace to burn and a blower would then push the heat to the house through large ducts. There was a wooden coal room next to the furnace. Sometimes I had to shovel coal from the coal room to fill the stoker bin.

In the dream, I was shoveling coal into the stoker bin to keep the furnace fire going. I was doing the best I could but not keeping up. No matter how hard I shoveled, there was not enough coal in the stoker. The fire in the furnace was flickering and almost out. I was in a panic. And then the fire in the furnace went out completely.

At that moment, a very cold chill went from my scalp to my toes. I woke up shivering and cold. I pulled the covers over me, hugged my pillow and drifted back to sleep. The dream continued. In the dream I saw myself as a young boy cowering under a blanket sitting on top of a heat register between our living and dining room. But there was no heat. The fire was out.

I was afraid and angry because no matter how much coal I shoveled it was never enough. But then in my dream, there was a candle and it was lit and glowing. It came from my mind and started to warm me all over. I was happy to have the candle there but was still afraid because I left the fire go out and might be scolded. I awakened from the dream for the second time feeling puzzled and curious.

My interpretation of this dream was that the coal shoveling represented my compulsive efforts to keep everyone else warm and happy, what is sometimes referred to as "codependency". It represented how hard I was trying to please others. But no matter how hard I worked at feeding coal into the stoker, the furnace went out anyway! It was not enough. I was not enough. I was never enough! This resulted in feelings of inferiority, inadequacy, hurt, fear. Naturally, I was expecting some reciprocal understanding and approval. The result was hurt and anger.

But now at age forty-four, something was happening inside. There was a light, there was some understanding and warmth that were helping me see. But I was frightened. After this dream, my stomach physically hurt, it was in a knot. When I pressed my hand on my solar plexus, it was literally tender for one or two days after the dream. Something deep inside me wanted to be heard. It was angry about being ignored. The light was lit but could easily be blown out.

* * * * *

During the years from 1988 to 1993, I realized the wonderful change that was coming slowly from within. I began to plan some vacations on my own. I went to Key West, Florida two different times and each time stayed in a "clothing optional" gay owned bed and breakfast. Each Bed and Breakfast had a swimming pool area with a Jacuzzi and places to lounge and meet other men.

There, for a few days, I could be myself without shame or guilt. I could be honest and felt at home in my body. I could meet and talk to other gay men, some of whom were also married or had been married.

One of the men I met was an Episcopal priest from Philadelphia. He and I talked about how he could integrate being gay and Christian. He seemed to be able to reconcile this tension within himself and was happy. I was far from being able to integrate being gay and Christian but just talking to that priest helped me consider that it might be possible to do so. This discussion and experiences with other gay men helped me accept myself and my feelings. I was starting to surrender to the truth in my body.

My conflicted feeling about marriage and family continued to weigh heavily on me. During that time, I wrote the following in my journal. It was in the form of a letter I wrote to my family but never gave to them:

Dear Family: I will no longer pretend to be what I am not. I will no longer apologize for what I feel. I will no longer sneak and hide to protect you from feelings. I am gay. That means simply I desire to make love to men and have them as my closest friends. This is opposite of what society expects and approves of. I know this is judged to be immoral and wrong by many religions. I accept full responsibility for choosing to act on my orientation.

I could choose to continue to pretend. I could choose to keep up appearances. I could choose to hide. But, that is emotional suicide. And that very well could lead to physical suicide. Is it better for me to kill myself and end it all? Would you rather have me dead than gay? Perhaps that would be easier for all to cope with. I think it comes down to that. I don't want to do that. I don't want to end this life, but at times I do contemplate that seriously. A traffic fatality could be just right.

Chapter Ten

Crossing The Bridge—Revisited

In 1988, my wife and I were living on Everett Drive in Norton with our two children. My son Leif was 14 and my daughter Jennifer was 16. I had a busy psychotherapy private practice in the Norton and Akron community and my wife was in graduate school to become a licensed counselor.

One cool spring evening, I took my motorcycle on the road for a long drive. I heard the hum of my motorcycle as I was riding the open road. Damn, it was running smoothly from the tune up the week before. I loved that beautiful bike and the freedom it gave me. When I would ride it out on the open road, I felt free from the constrictions of my home and church life. I felt free from all the shoulds of life. I was in touch with the road, life and myself. But in real life, I was not free.

The wind was blowing in my face that evening as my bike moved toward its destinations. The air dried the tears forming in my eyes. I noticed some daffodils in full bloom in a yard along the road. So beautiful. They seemed to nod and bow their heads reverently as I drove by.

I felt the despair of my life so poignantly that the usual concern for how suicide might affect others faded and I was focused on escaping the trap I was in and stopping the emotional pain. At that moment nothing else seemed to matter—nothing. Oh how I loved my wife and children and did not want to hurt them. But it seemed I could not go on.

Given my self judgments and projections of rejection if I came out, I felt I had no choice. To the fearful, lonely and angry wounded child within me, suicide by "accident" seemed like the only way out. How could I have gotten to this place in my life journey?

I turned on Greenwich Road. The bridge was just a short distance ahead. I wondered why time was going so slowly? It seemed it was taking an eternity to get there. Eternity? Maybe I had already done it and this was death—was I already on the other side? If so, is this all there is?

No, I must still be here. I could feel my hands gripping the handlebars tightly. I felt the vibrations of my motorcycle on my rear end. I am still here. Troubled as I was, it felt good to be here, alive in that moment. My heart was beating rapidly as the moment to decide arrived. My breathing was more rapid. Where was I? What was I going to do?

From somewhere out there or inside me, came the moment of grace. Something greater than myself. Something beyond reason. There was the courage to say no to death and yes to life. It was an existential defining moment—the desire to be rather than not be, to live rather than die.

And now I was at the bridge. I could hear the traffic zooming underneath. Big semi trucks rumbling by carrying their cargo. Cars were whizzing by. I took a deep breath and stared straight ahead. I grasped the handle bars of my bike ever so tightly and drove across that bridge to the other side…such an utterly simple act---going to the other side, so simple and yet so profound. I had crossed that bridge and others many times before. But this time was different. This time was special.

How did I cross that bridge? Was the answer "blowing in the wind" as the folk song says. Or was it the respect of the daffodils bowing to me as I passed them along Greenwich road? Or was it the good bodily feeling of being grounded and in touch with the handlebars of the motorcycle running on the good earth? Was I temporarily in the hands of the Source of Life? Did it carry me over?

I don't know. The what or why questions are interesting but in a way rude and obscene. The word labels mean nothing, my belief about it is not important. What was important was the felt presence of something wonderful—grace, life energy from the Dynamic Ground, which had been repressed since birth! Something from the Source of Life itself.

A part of me wishes I could write and speak of this moment in a rational and matter of fact way. But I cannot. Even today I cannot write or speak of this moment without tears welling up in my eyes. Even now twenty-two years later, the tears are flowing.

No wonder I had to pull off the road on the other side and let my emotions release. There was no dam strong enough to hold them back. With the emotional release came release of shame and guilt and then affirmation of my being, my authentic and loving core and its goodness. There was no judgment. No guilt. No shame. Just joy in the moment. This was salvation for me. It had nothing to do with finding a religion and everything to do with finding me. Becoming honest, clean and true to myself, my human self.

The crossing only took twenty seconds but seemed like twenty minutes. However, living out the change has been life long and tested many times. I had survived my "dark night of the soul" and emerged on the other side distinctly different. The self-destructive forces of self-hatred, denial, repression and fear were being disarmed.

Choosing to live as I am, honestly, freely and openly continued a process within me that started after the seminar in Chicago many years earlier. It was a process of self acceptance, self loving and self affirmation. The process was continued by my cathartic exclamation at Race Point Beach on Cape Cod that "I am gay!" Being able to scream out my truth, call that fear by name and affirm my life and being was nothing short of bliss.

I now believe that what was really behind the bridge incident is that I was very angry inside, not because of any real or actual rejection or condemnation by anyone, but because I projected my own self-hatred for having same sex desires and acting on them. I projected that anger outward and assumed others, like my family and church, would condemn me as harshly as I condemned myself.

Did I know that "they" would condemn me or judge me? I didn't know that for sure. There were some reasons to suspect they might judge me based on their typical reactions to the unknown. But, there was also evidence that some would try to understand and be accepting and loving. I ignored that. I was willing to assume the worst and act as though it was fact.

My belief and projection process were so powerful I was almost willing to bet my life on a perception that I could never be loved as a gay man, and that I would be rejected by everyone that mattered to me! After all I was different,

I had a secret. I now thank the Source of Life, The Dynamic Ground of Being that I did not bet on fear and shame that spring evening.

In truth, I loved and respected myself. I thought I was wonderful. I thought I was special and loved. That's why I wanted to live.

Often after taking a step forward and seeing things differently, a time of testing that new understanding comes along. There is a situation that is a temptation to return to the comfort of the old, worn way of thinking. My test came only three months after the bridge crossing.

After the bridge crossing, I sold my Honda 550 and bought a used Kawasaki 650 cc motorcycle so I could have more power on the freeway! It was a beautiful bike and I enjoyed riding the open roads. It's an exhilarating experience of freedom like nothing else one can know.

I've noticed that often after a life-changing experience, life brings us another challenge that tests the tenacity of that change. And so it was.

It was June 25th, 1988. I was riding my "new" motorcycle through the small town of Lodi, Ohio, about twenty miles from my home. It was over 100 degrees Fahrenheit that day as the sun beat down on me.

About 1 p.m., as I passed through this small village, a tree branch fell directly on my bike. I was thrown off of my motorcycle and landed on my side in someone's yard. I was scraped up and bleeding and my shoulder was in excruciating pain.

Even though I was in pain and stunned while laying in that yard, I looked up at the tree overhead. I looked at the branch; it had green leaves on it. It was not dead. I wanted to see if part of the tree was dead. It wasn't. I was hoping it was, and then it would seem like a natural event. Neither the tree nor the branch was dead. The only explanation I could think of was that the branch fell due to the high heat that day. Or of course, the act of God explanation again. Already, I was trying to find meaning in this event.

The ambulance came in about ten minutes and took me to the small Lodi Medical Center where an emergency room doctor tried to get my dislocated shoulder back in the socket. I was turned in a way I could see him looking in a medical book. I thought, "Is he reading—put tab A into socket B?" Maybe he was a resident in training.

After it was clear to me he did not know what he was doing, I said, "Hey Doc! This is my god-damn shoulder and it really hurts, call someone in that can do it!" He did so immediately and the specialist arrived in about fifteen minutes. Thankfully the specialist knew how to work with my shoulder and get it re-positioned. I was soon bandaged up and released with my arm in a sling. I was able to return home that same day. Carolyn came to get me in the car. She was very nurturing, caring and willing to help me start the healing process.

I went to physical therapy for six weeks or so and the therapists did what they could with heat, electrical stimulation and movement. Yet at the end of the therapy, I could not lift my left arm above a forty degree angle without severe pain.

An orthopedic specialist I consulted for a second opinion told me the large deltoid muscle was paralyzed and it might take up to a year for it to return to normal, if it did so at all. He said if it did not heal in a year, it would likely never heal.

This frightened me and motivated me to take charge of my recovery. I got a membership in a local gym/natatorium and worked through the pain until ten months later my arm could move normally with full range of motion. I used swimming and the Nautilus machines to exercise. The story of my recovery is in itself a remarkable journey but one I will not belabor here.

I would sometimes drive my motorcycle fast and recklessly as if to challenge fate and maybe live out a death wish. But as far as I can tell, this motorcycle accident had nothing to do with carelessness due to a subconscious death wish. I had to reflect though on the possible meaning of this accident.

Was it chance, a roll of the dice? Or, was the man-God in the sky trying to tell me that exploring same-sex intimacy was wrong? Was this an angry God-parent punishing his prodigal child? Part of my mind was eager to co-opt this traditional idea and use it to guilt and shame me all the way back to the God-understanding of my childhood.

And maybe if I did return to my childhood God, my deltoid muscle would heal. And if I didn't maybe I would be paralyzed for life. It was tempting to resurrect this traditional interpretation. I could make a bargain with this god. But the temptation did not last long.

I knew I had struggled too long and come too far in accepting myself to return to the old ways of believing, satisfying as they might have been to my bad boy morality. I thought, if this is how the source of Life, the God of the universe operates, in a capricious and punishing way, then I cannot trust or love that God.

I had just crossed the bridge into a life of freedom and release from guilt and shame about who I was and I was not going to look back! I had not come out to my family yet but it was only a matter of time. Tempting as it was, I did not return to that way of thinking and believing. And, my deltoid muscle did heal in time and I have full use of that arm and shoulder. Today at the gym I can lift thirty pounds of free weights with each arm at the same time.

As I began living on the other side of the bridge I became poignantly aware of the beautiful and loving little boy I had abandoned by trying to please others. That little boy had feelings in his body that were labeled bad and sinful and so had to be repressed. Finding him was the key to my recovery and re-integration

My child within was indeed lonely. I began to look more for friendship than sex. Toward the end of 1988 I met Tom through an ad he had placed in a gay newspaper. I met him at his home several times and began to like him a lot. He was single, educated and mature. There was some sexual attraction but more than that there was some emotional intimacy that met a deep need.

I was learning that the sexual and the emotional could come together in a relationship/friendship. That was a completely new learning for me and changed everything. When sex was casual, quick and just physical release, it lacked meaning and significance. It could easily have become an addiction or just an affair. Certainly, it did not make sense to disrupt my marriage and family life for casual sex.

If I had been a straight man who enjoyed occasional sex with men as an aside, I likely would have stayed married and kept my secret sexual trysts secret. If I were a bisexual man who could respond physically and emotionally to both men and women, I likely would have chosen to remain married.

But something fundamentally different was starting to happen this time. In my Journal I wrote about this new discovery. Speaking of my new friend I wrote:

"I find myself reaching out to Tom, wanting to be with him. I want to say I love him but am scared to do so. We really don't know each other that well. It was only a week or so that we had met. And yet what I am aware of is the very strong attraction. The feeling of loving and caring and wanting to talk to and share.

And now there is a knot in my stomach again. It's a big one and it doesn't want to go away this time. Its something I don't remember feeling before. What happens when you have looked for something, searched in vain for 40 years and you find it?

What happens when you find it and it feels good? You know you want to keep it. You know you don't want it to go away. And yet you know, things may not work out with that person. But maybe another. It's the kind of thing one might up and leave it all. Might do something irrational. That scares me. Like I could just announce it to the world and let happen what happens. My logic says don't do that, it will only cause great pain for other people. It will hurt and disappoint and confuse them. And those I love.

Something new wants to emerge, but I won't let it. I strain to hold back and keep it in. To do so I must deny it is there. It's like I'm a snail trying to get out of its shell and pushing and pushing to get out. But scared a big bird will snoop down and gobble me up the moment I am out. HELP! Where is there a birthing room that is safe? Will anyone be there for me? "

While the relationship with this friend did not continue for various reasons, my time with him and the bringing together of sexual and emotional intimacy was an important new learning. When I knew that it was possible to feel a wholeness and completeness with a man, I also discovered that I needed that in my life. It was the blending of these energies that felt like a coming home experience. This was the missing piece in my puzzle. And this is what is so difficult for non-gay people to comprehend.

I was born a gay male, period. That's it. That's the truth. It is not a "lifestyle" that I got snared into by any devil or gay recruiter. It is not a mistake or an illness that needs fixing. I needed to please others so much I would *never* freely choose a role or lifestyle that has been demonized by society. And, it is not at its core about sex. It's about love. It's about loving someone that I choose to love and loving them freely, naturally.

Like almost all gay children growing up in a straight society, I was abused. No, not sexually or physically abused or molested. I was abused by my culture, the pervasive assumptions that since I had feelings of attraction to the same sex that there was something wrong with me. That I was in some way sinful, sick, silly or sinister.

I had to recover from a form of Posttraumatic Stress Disorder—the stress of trying to be accepted in a hostile culture that teased, cajoled and subtly or not so subtly demeaned who I was. I was nurtured in a family and culture that did not understand or accept me as I was. For the most part it was done from ignorance and not malice. I understand why some young gay children and teens are so devastated by this hostile environment that they commit suicide.

I want to be clear; I do not blame straight people for this situation entirely. They too are victims of the cultural prejudice. Many straight people are actually more homoanxious than homophobic. Some of the most homophobic and culturally abusive people I know are gay people suffering from P.T.S.D. as they internalize society's fears.

A few years after this bridge crossing, I used the analogy of singing my song to those I loved. In my journal I wrote:

"If I do not make a clear and open choice to sing the song God gave me here on this earth then I will choose to sing it in my death and that would be easier in many ways."

Mennonites have pride in their four part harmony singing. And for good reason. It is beautiful to hear. To sing out of key or harmony was frowned upon. It was clear who could and who could not "carry a tune. " Mother was a good singer, so was my brother Dale. Dad was sometimes asked not to sing as loudly because he sang out of tune. I was told my singing was often "flat". Sorry. But that did not keep me from joining in because I loved to sing. I even played a guitar for a number of years.

My song was out of harmony with those around me. And yet I have found a chorus of other men who sing like I do. We are often off beat and hear a different drummer. And yet, to each other, we know the music and the words and the beat goes on. Even if some of us are out of tune.

I have a wonderful song to sing. It is my song. I will sing it out loud. I will sing it Keith. I will sing it Eric. I will sing it Rich. I will sing it Jesus. I will sing it mom and dad, brother and sister. I will sing it Carolyn, Leif, and Jennifer. I will sing my song because I love and respect the God who made me. And I will sing even if it seems out of tune.

Chapter Eleven

Valentines Day

Carolyn and I took the kids to Cancun, Mexico, to our time-share condo during the holiday vacation break in January of 1989. We were there with them for one week and then the kids returned with some friends we had met there. Carolyn and I stayed an extra 4 or 5 days to give us some time together.

Carolyn and I talked about a lot of things. It was quite obvious that I was going through some kind of mid-life crisis. I would go for long walks, journal on my laptop and show other signs of depression like irritability and moodiness.

Carolyn and I spent time sharing thoughts and feelings about the marriage. We reviewed the positives and negatives of our relationship over the years and how our relationship with our parents and siblings shaped us. We shared how our feelings about our bodies and sex were influenced by the attitudes of our parents, our church and society. But at the end of the discussions, there was something that did not feel right between us.

What was lacking in our sharing was that I did not disclose to Carolyn what was really going on regarding my experiences with men. It seems we talked around that issue. We both needed to face this reality.

I hinted at this issue by sharing about some of my early feelings for guys….but I was not quite ready yet to disclose explicitly. I remember being very despondent on the plane home from Cancun. I knew I would have to find a way to come out to Carolyn fully and soon.

On Valentines Day, 1989, I got ready to go to Canton to do my consulting work at the drug abuse prevention agency where I was employed part-time as their consulting psychologist.

As I was walking out the door, Carolyn gave me a Valentines Day card. I thanked her but decided to read the card on my drive to Canton since I was running late. That was a mistake.

On one side of the card, which I still have, is a note from Carolyn. I started to read it as I was driving. She wrote:

"On this eve of St. Valentines Day, I think back over the last weeks and months of our lives. We are changing, growing each in our own ways. To me this is exciting, scary, painful and wonderful! I feel that I have learned to know you better and deeply respect you. And lastly (this is the real scary part) you have the freedom from this marriage if your changing so needs it. This is not what I would desire and it would be painful, however I would prefer you to be free and happy than bound and angry. I have really enjoyed sharing time, love and caring with you."

Tears filled my eyes so much I could hardly see to drive. I pulled to the side of the road to dry my eyes so I could see to drive. I was able to get to the agency. My boss at the agency was somewhat aware of my marital situation and was understanding. She suggested that if I could stay and have supervision sessions with three of the counselors until noon then I could leave early. This was a huge relief.

On the drive home, I felt both deep sadness and joy. My head was spinning. What was I going to do and when? There was love for Carolyn who was willing to put my happiness above hers. I wondered if Carolyn really meant what she wrote in her card and if so, would I take her up on the offer to release me. Part of me wanted to answer Carolyn's offer to release me from the marriage with an immediate "YES!" But I just couldn't imagine actually leaving her and the children. Hardly anyone in either of our extended families got divorced.

When I got home I hugged Carolyn and thanked her for the card and what she wrote. I told her we needed to talk. We decided to go to dinner that Friday evening. I felt closer to Carolyn than I had in years. It seems I could now begin to feel something for her that had been missing. And yet the closeness had to do with her unselfishness and the freedom she had offered.

Napoleon was finally defeated at the Battle of Waterloo, Brussels in June of 1815. It seems ironic, if not appropriate, that Carolyn and I decided to eat that evening at The Waterloo restaurant on Waterloo Road in Akron, Ohio. Perhaps it was an appropriate choice because the hope that I could continue living as a closeted gay man would be finally defeated that February of 1989. After twenty years of struggle the forces of deception and dishonesty would be defeated by the simple truth.

As usual, it was a busy night at the Waterloo restaurant. We were seated right smack in the middle of the lower part of the restaurant, not very private. We were in a fishbowl. I had hoped for one of the more private booths on the upper level but those were taken. I was very frightened; so much was at stake, and the final outcome unknown.

I was anxious and restless during the first and second dinner courses because I didn't know how Carolyn would respond. I ordered their good meatloaf and mashed potatoes entrée. Carolyn had one of their specialty salads with grilled chicken. It seemed the service was unusually slow that evening. Or was it that I was just nervous to get done with dinner and get this over with.

While talking to Carolyn and eating I was thinking, "Would Carolyn be angry? Would she ask me to move out and file for divorce? Would she try to turn our two children against me?" Our daughter Jennifer was seventeen and a senior in high school. Our son Leif was fifteen and a sophomore. Both were attending a Mennonite church private high school about forty-five minutes from our home. Leif would soon be sixteen and start to drive.

But the deepest immediate concern I had that evening, because I felt it was Carolyn's most likely and understandable response, was that she would blame herself for my being gay. Over the years when we would discuss our problems, Carolyn seemed too ready to blame herself for situations for which we both were clearly responsible.

The Waterloo was famous for their "big apple" dessert. It is an apple cobbler type dessert served warm with a scoop of cinnamon ice cream. It was served in a special ceramic dish, which customers could take home. We decided to share the big apple dessert since it was large.

When we were done with dessert and I had my coffee refilled, I knew the time had come. I just had to say it. I could delay no longer. I looked at Carolyn and said, "Carolyn, I want to say again how much I appreciated your Valentine's Day card. I was very moved by your saying you would be willing to end our relationship if that is what I need to be happy." Carolyn nodded. I continued, "As you know I have been very troubled lately as you said in your card." I was starting to repeat myself and delaying getting out what I knew was coming. For so many years I denied my truth to myself and others but now was the time.

"Carolyn," I stammered, "There is something I need to tell you. Do you recall the time seven or eight years ago when Art came out to me and our small group at church?" She nodded yes. "And that evening after I talked with Art and the kids were in bed, we sat on the couch in our living room in our home on Neptune St., and I told you I was struggling with feelings of attraction to men?"

She said she remembered. But there was an "oh no, not that!" expression on her face. I continued, "Those feelings have never gone away and I now believe that I am bisexual for sure and probably gay."

"How do you know this for sure?" she asked.

"This is very difficult to say to you, but I have had some sexual experiences with men over the last few years that convinces me I am gay." Carolyn looked surprised and worried but let me continue. "For example," I said, "when I went to Key West last fall I stayed at a gay bed and breakfast and had sex with men while there. And there have been other times and places. I have been living with this turmoil and stress which has been getting worse. It is this struggle inside me that has been causing my unhappiness and depression."

I was extremely tense because I had just admitted infidelity. Carolyn had never asked me about my being involved with anyone else because I don't think she suspected I would ever do that. Now would be the moment for Carolyn to ask for a divorce if she was going to do so. She didn't and I was greatly relieved. I folded and refolded my napkin numerous times to distract myself. I noticed most of the other customers had finished their dinners and were leaving. The staff was cleaning up for the evening. But I was not done.

"And what I want you to understand most of all," I said, "is that my being gay is not your fault. It's not anyone's fault. The problems we have had over the years with intimacy have been mostly the result of my being gay and not anything you have done or not done."

Carolyn listened to my words but I don't think she could fully hear or accept them inside. How could she? After twenty years of knowing me in one way, as her straight husband and now she was told it wasn't so! Carolyn said she had been afraid I might be struggling with those feelings but I can't recall if she said how she sensed that.

The rest of our conversation is a blur. I don't remember what more we said at that time. I could see she was upset by what I just said. Her eyes were moist and there was tension in her face. I believe Carolyn and I had some discussion about how our families would react if and when I came out to them. It was scary for both of us.

I hated to see Carolyn upset and tearful! I typically felt guilty for causing her tears and would try to comfort her and smooth things over. She did not like to argue and when we disagreed often said "its just not worth fighting over." So I would often ignore my feelings and needs and our discussions would end without resolution.

But this time had to be different. My "no more nails" feelings of guilt and shame from childhood had to go. My compulsive need to please others at the expense of my own needs had to stop. This is what it meant when I crossed that bridge last year. This time I knew I had to stay with what I knew and work out what needed to be done from there. No more apologies for being who I was. And no more abandoning myself.

By this time I had at least three cups of coffee if not four, which is enough to keep me awake a long time. But we were both exhausted. Most others in the restaurant had left and it was past time for us to leave as well. The waiter looked perplexed. They wanted to bus the table. We left. There was a respectful silence as we drove home. Nothing more needed to be said. I reached over and grasped Carolyn's hand as I drove our blue Pontiac Grand Am home that night. We knew everything had changed. Would this new truth set us free?

This information about my sexual orientation began an extremely painful time of awakening for Carolyn as a person and for us as a couple. We decided to seek some counseling both individually and together to help us decide what to do. This was somewhat helpful but it was our journey and we had to eventually make the difficult decisions. It would have been even more helpful for me to have a psychologist who was gay and out.

We decided that we would stay together at least for awhile to see if the marriage could continue but that in any event we would disclose this information to our children and we would do it together.

This disclosure to Carolyn was painful but helpful in many ways. At least we could begin to face the truth together rather than playing games. It brought us closer in that we had a common problem to work on—what to do now that we acknowledged we were in a mixed orientation marriage.

We made contact with other couples in similar situations. I made contact with the GAMMA—Gay and Married Men's Association in Washington, D.C. I talked with one of their leaders on the phone and he was helpful. We also met once with a local support group of other mixed orientation couples.

Carolyn, for her part, made contact with the Straight Spouse Support Network, www.straightspouse.org nationally and locally. She read the book *The Other Side of the Closet* by Amity Pierce Buxton, a book about mixed orientation marriages. She had contact with the author for a period of time and considered writing her own memoir.

Chapter Twelve
Family Disclosures

Another story is interwoven with my coming out process. My brother Dale and his wife live in Springfield, Ohio. They have two children, Eric and Joanie. My brother is now a retired school teacher and principal.

Eric graduated with honors from a religiously conservative church college near his home near Dayton, Ohio in 1987. After graduating he decided to enroll in The University of Akron to work on a Master's Degree in Psychology. At family gatherings, Eric and I liked to talk about many things, particularly a more liberal understanding of religious faith. Eric is a very talented musician in both writing and piano performance.

Eric asked if he could stay with our family in Akron while in graduate school at The University of Akron. Carolyn and I gladly consented as we had an extra bedroom. We enjoyed having Eric live with us and he and I got into discussions about psychology and religion.

As I observed Eric in our home, I did notice that he seemed troubled and depressed. Something was bothering him. I noticed he did not seem to have much of a social life. He would leave the house in the evenings sometimes and come back later but did not talk about friends he had been with. He said some things that made me wonder if he might be struggling with the same kind of feelings that I had for men.

One Sunday afternoon Eric asked to talk privately with me. I had just come out to Carolyn at our dinner on Waterloo Road about six weeks earlier but had not disclosed my being gay to Eric yet at this time. Eric and I went to my office close by where we would not be interrupted. He spoke slowly and deliberately.

"I have this good friend and we are not getting along right now, he said. And, I have very strong feelings for this friend and like this friend a lot. I guess I need to tell you that this friend is a guy and I am gay. I have had feelings for guys since I was a young boy. I had crushes on male teachers growing up and other men I saw on TV."

In a recent email to me about his time of staying with our family, Eric said, "The first year of graduate school I was going through the dual but linked process of separating from fundamentalist Christianity and coming out to myself as gay."

After listening awhile to his process of coming out to himself, I took a restroom break and got some water. I was nervous when I came back into the room and sat on the couch.

I looked at Eric directly and said, "Eric, I have something to share with you also. Even though I am married with two children, I too have struggled with feeling attracted to guys and have had some same sex experiences in the last year."

Eric shifted in his chair and said, "does Carolyn know?" I said, "I just told her clearly about six weeks ago but we have not told the kids yet. We plan to do that soon."

He said, "Well Jim, I did notice on your computer that you were part of an online bulletin board men's community that was gay. I thought perhaps you were there because of your work with gays as a psychologist. But, I see now it was more than that."

I acknowledged that I had met some gay men on the internet and made some other friends there. Bulletin Boards were just starting to be available on the internet at that time.

Our mutual disclosure brought Eric and me closer emotionally. There was quite a bit of drama around our home during this time with both of us coming out simultaneously!

Eric needed support in coming out to his parents. He knew it would be very painful for them to hear he was gay. Within a week or so Eric did tell his parents he was gay over the phone. And it *was* quite upsetting to them.

Since his coming out to them, Eric and his parents have worked very hard at mutual understanding and respect. I respect the difficult process they have been through in trying to bridge the chasm between them over this issue.

Eric now lives in Boston with his partner Jordan. They have been together ten years and, in the last few years, have visited Eric's parents together at holiday times. Eric's parents have also visited them in the home Eric and Jordan bought together in 2007.

* * * * *

In October of 1989, about a month after the 7.1 magnitude earthquake hit San Francisco, the American Association of Marriage and Family Therapists met in that city for its annual convention. I wanted to attend because there was a series of seminars for those interested in gay/lesbian/bi/transgender issues.

I had a telephone contact with Keith, a gay Mennonite marriage and family therapist from Iowa, who was going to be at the convention. He had been married many years and had 4 grown children. He and his wife had decided to divorce some years ago. Carolyn was interested in meeting and talking to him about his experiences.

The convention was significant for several reasons. Carolyn and I found talking to Keith and hearing his experience to be a reality shock. He told us how difficult it was for him and his wife to separate and divorce. But, his ex wife went on with her life and was doing well. I felt a closeness and bond with Keith because of our similar backgrounds and situations.

Keith and I spent one evening walking the streets of San Francisco and talking. I got back to the hotel about 2 a.m. When I returned Carolyn had taken off her wedding ring and had it lying on the desk with a note saying it was over between us. It was a very painful night for both of us, with little sleep. No way was I ready to accept my marriage was over! And yet I knew also that it was.

Carolyn observed how long I primped in getting ready to meet Keith that evening. I fussed with my hair and clothes much more that usual. She could see that the kind of feelings guys have when dating a girl were the same as if two guys had feelings for each. It seemed to me something shifted in her understanding about what being gay was all about.

During one of the plenary sessions of the convention which Carolyn and

I attended together, The San Francisco Gay Men's Chorus gave a concert. I was awed to see one hundred plus out gay men dressed in suits and ties and singing beautiful music together. What a positive image it burned in my consciousness. No words could do what seeing and hearing them did for me that night. They dedicated their songs to chorus members and other friends who had died of AIDS in the previous year. After the concert Carolyn and I went to the front of the room to thank the men for their music and to talk to some of them.

After returning from San Francisco, Carolyn and I decided it was time to tell our children. My daughter Jennifer had just started her first year of college at Conrad Grebel College on the campus of the large University of Waterloo in Waterloo, Ontario Canada. My son Leif, was a sophomore at our church high school in Kidron, Ohio.

One afternoon after Leif got home from school and had some time to relax, I told him that his mom and I wanted to talk to him in the living room. He knew something big was up because we *never* used the living room except for more formal visits or special occasions.

Carolyn and I sat at either end of the lovely new couch with beautiful flowered upholstery. Leif sat on the floor in front of us in a semi-lotus position. I had thought about how I wanted to phrase what I said to Leif. I wanted him to see me first as a man and then as gay. I began speaking slowly and deliberately with tension in my voice:

"There is some information that your mom and I think you should have at this time. I have decided to share this with you because above all I feel that it is important that people be honest with each other about what is happening, and also I am sharing because I love you and care for you a lot.

Slowly, over the last years, I have come to accept myself as a man. And, I have come to accept myself as a man who is gay."

Leif and I had good eye contact with each other so I continued:

"As you might imagine, this has been very difficult for me because of how society and the church looks at being gay, but I have had to be honest with myself. We want to know what your thoughts and feelings are about this and hope we can share."

Leif listened intently and looked at me and said "Its o.k. Dad, I understand."

I continued: "This is one of the reasons why your mom and I went for counseling, and why I have been close to Eric (my nephew who was living with us at the time). Eric and I have talked a lot but we have not been intimate with each other."

It was then Carolyn's turn to speak. " Leif, you probably wonder how this affects us as a couple, she said. We want you to know that we have talked about divorce and that it might happen some months down the road. However, we have been working on our relationship and are trying to see if it makes sense for us to stay together. Whatever happens, if we do divorce, we will still be your parents and love you and we hope we can be friendly with each other even if we divorce."

I did not want to offer easy reassurance or false hope so I said, "That's no guarantee, but we hope we could be friendly in a divorce."

Carolyn was supportive of me by adding: "We have both grown in this. Maybe you have noticed your dad has been different, not as angry and more himself lately. I have grown a lot, too."

Leif responded to this by looking at me directly and saying, "Yes, I have noticed that you do not yell at me as much and that you are less angry. That's been good."

This felt very good to me that he noticed the change in me. I knew I had at times been quite irritable and moody. And with Jennifer away now at university, I think Leif got more of my frustration than he deserved.

I said, "I am glad you have noticed that because I don't want you to be afraid of me. Leif, I honestly believe that very likely one of the reasons I have been so critical of you and have been angry at you was to hide my fear of you knowing me too well and finding out my secret. Now, we don't need to hide anymore."

I noticed that Leif was looking directly at me and that he had a few tears in his eyes. I wanted him to understand more of what he no doubt noticed. So I said, "All this is why your mom and I have had so many long walks, and why I go out sometimes. We have shared many painful feelings. I go out to be with my friends. Sometimes I go to a bar where mostly gay guys hang out. I enjoy being with them and sometimes play pool."

Carolyn was calm and composed so far but the strain in her face became noticeable. She added: "We have not told many others yet except our therapists because we wanted you to know first." Leif nodded in appreciation.

I felt a huge relief just to get through this disclosure. I said, "Wow. This wasn't as hard as I thought it was going to be. I was really anxious and got awake early this morning thinking about this."

Leif smiled broadly and said, "It feels good to get it out, doesn't it?"

Yes, it certainly did feel good and my wonderful son knew just what I needed to hear. We hugged and held each other.

Several weeks later Carolyn, Leif and I went to visit Jennifer at her school in Waterloo, Ontario. Our main purpose was to tell her what we had told Leif. She came to our motel room and sat in the middle of one of the beds. When I started to tell her about my being gay, she moved back on the bed to rest against the headboard. She listened and did not say much.

Jennifer asked what it might mean for the marriage, and we told her we were not sure. Naturally, she was concerned and stunned by this disclosure.

Jennifer and Carolyn had some time to talk alone that afternoon. Jennifer came home for Christmas vacation and spent most of the time with her mom and brother. I don't recall much interaction between us regarding my being gay during that time.

After the convention, Keith and I visited each other several times. We had intense times sharing and bonding together. He was about 5 years older than I and very nurturing. I felt safe with him and free to just be myself with another man for the first time in my life.

The first weekend in December of 1989, just before moving away from my home, I visited Keith in his small but lovely home in Ames, Iowa. Saturday evening, after a day of grocery shopping, baking cookies and being very domestic, Keith and I had some time to talk.

Enya's beautiful and enchanting *Waterfall* cd was playing softly in the background. Keith was on the couch and I was in front of him, leaning back against him so he could have his arms around me, embracing me from behind. Keith could tell I was very troubled as I was facing my own decision of whether to move away from Carolyn and the children or to stay.

I said, "Keith, now that I have come out to Carolyn, my children and my family. I feel so much better and freer. I feel like I am me and can love myself as I am. But, moving away and leaving the family I love so much just breaks my heart. I know eventually they will be OK and survive. But, I feel so responsible for their happiness. It seems I can't win either way. If I stay and pretend to be straight I abandon myself again. If I leave I feel I am abandoning them."

"Jim", Keith said, "I can't tell you what to do. Only you can decide what you need to do and when. But for me, he continued, I had to make a change and leave my wife. I could not go on living a divided life. It was extremely painful."

His voice began to break up and he struggled to continue sharing without crying. There was a long silence. No words were needed. He breathed very deeply and we began to breathe in sync, inhaling deeply and releasing our breaths slowly and deeply. Keith's loving arms reached over my shoulders and embraced me in a hug. He held me tightly and it felt so good.

"But," Keith continued haltingly, "As painful as it was for me and all of my family, I do not regret leaving. I had to be free to live honestly as I was."

With that I began to sob so deeply I couldn't cry. I held my breath as long as I could and then gasped deeply for the next breath.

Keith continued to hold me until I totally left go and left myself melt into his affirming and loving arms.

Keith was not afraid of my pain. He could be a mid-wife to help me through the travail of this birth. He had been there for himself in his own pain so he could be there for me in mine. My pain was far too deep for words. There was nothing to do but notice it, honor it and let it go. Yes, I had crossed the bridge of suicide but I didn't know it would be this painful or perhaps I would have chosen differently. But, I was still glad I chose to live. It could only get better, I thought. I returned home to Ohio with a clear sense of what was likely ahead.

The last day of the year, Carolyn and I had some time to talk again. We agreed together that given where each of us was in our lives at the time, it was best for us to separate. We agreed that Carolyn would take Jennifer back to school the next day and I would pack some things and go to a motel. That night I wrote about our talk in my journal:

I sobbed deeply after our talk and felt an inner aching too deep for words. It felt good to feel so deeply. I knew and know that what I felt was so basic and fundamental. It was like I opened up my soul and experienced my wound directly, without defenses. And, it did not blow me away. I was o.k. Carolyn could understand that it was not her. That I was not angry with her. But rather that I had discovered a truth that was core.

Chapter Thirteen

A New Beginning

On January 1, 1990 I began my own "gay 90's". I packed some of my clothes and belongings in several suitcases and drove the five miles to what was then a Knights Inn Motel in Wadsworth. Perfect. This good knight was very tired! He needed to say goodnight to taking care of everyone else. No longer could he be the "Knight in Shining Armor" for others. He needed a place to regroup.

Sir James, not the pious St. James, signed in on the "weekly rate". The lady at the desk looked puzzled and could tell I was a very anxious and excited knight. It seemed it took her forever to process my credit card. I was now only moments away from the first minute of the rest of *my* life! Yes, my life, mine! "Ok, here is your key— room 132, just in the next unit over, and continental breakfast is from— blah blah blah."

I remember that moment I closed the heavy opaque drapes and double locked the door to my room. There was this wonderful silence. Here I am. I did it! This was the beginning of a new day, a new decade and a new life!

I took off all my clothes and skipped joyfully around the room half singing and half yelling the song from the Broadway musical *La Cage Aux Folles*. "I am what I am!! I don't want praise, I don't want pity, I bang my own drum, some think its noise, I think its pretty." It was a glorious release. This was the other side of the bridge. I was free from the closet, the games, the hiding, and the stress of living a divided life. I was finally taking responsibility for my own joy and happiness.

It was for this moment that I crossed over the bridge on my motorcycle that Spring day rather than run into it! It was for this moment that I had struggled so long and hard for the last twenty years! The travail was over in a way, but in another way it had only just begun.

This exhilaration lasted an hour or two. Then I began feeling the pain and anguish of moving away from my wife and children. I thought, "What had I done? Am I crazy? I must be very selfish!" That pain was now very poignant and never far from my consciousness. I sometimes had difficulty going to sleep at night.

Before I left home, I recorded some songs on a cassette tape as I knew I would need some self soothing. These were songs that spoke to my heart and soul. Some of the songs were "The Rose," "I Am What I Am," "Climb Every Mountain," songs from Enya's *Watermark* album, and a reading of *Desiderata* with symphonic background music. This music and words soothed my inner being and helped me heal. It also helped me go to sleep at night.

Within several weeks, I signed a one year lease for a one bedroom apartment in an apartment complex about 4 miles from my home. My apartment number was "2P". When telling friends my apartment number I sometimes joked, "2P or not 2P—that is the question."

I loved being able to arrange my things in *my* place and decorate it! This awakened my creative energy as nothing else could. This was the first time I had truly lived by myself, on my own! For the first time I was able to begin to get a sense of my own identity as an adult male and freely make choices.

When I was alone in my own apartment, I learned something important about myself I had never known. I discovered just what food meant to me and how I loved to cook when I took the time to do it right. I would alter and experiment with new ideas. Sometimes they bombed, other times they came out great. It was trial and error learning. I started trusting my intuitive instincts for food preparation.

Carolyn was a Home Economics teacher and so she naturally did the cooking for the family at home. I felt somewhat intimidated by her skills even though she always encouraged me when I would make foods at home. Yet I always felt like I was invading her domain. But that was clearly my issue and not hers!

Once I was on my own, I also found that preparing and serving good food was an important way I showed love to family and friends. That was one of the Mennonite values I kept. I would sometimes be frustrated and angry if friends I had invited over for dinner came late and the food would not taste as good since I had to keep it warm until they arrived.

Even after I moved out, Carolyn continued as the office manager of my practice and I saw her regularly when at work. I supported her as she went back to college. Over the next four years she completed a Master's Degree in Counseling and became a licensed Professional Clinical Counselor. Four or five years after our divorce, she re-married. She has her own private practice in counseling just down the street from my office and is a respected therapist in the community.

In 1988, I became aware of an organization called the Brethren Mennonite Council For Lesbian Gay Bisexual and Transgender Interests, http://www.bmclgbt.org. This is a wonderful supportive organization for LGBT individuals and their families who are in some way connected to the Church of the Brethren and Mennonite Church denominations worldwide.

This organization has grown significantly over the years and has many programs. It sponsors a biannual convention and yearly retreats for LGBT individuals and their families. I have attended some of the conventions and some of the "Connecting Families" annual retreats.

In April of 1990, Keith and I attended one of these retreats. It was a very significant time of healing for me. It helped me tremendously to know and feel love and affirmation from this community. During one of our worship events we sang the hymn, "There's A Wideness In God's Mercy." The second verse of this song is, "But we make God's love too narrow by false limits of our own, and we magnify his strictness with a zeal he will not own."

This was the message I needed to hear and know at that time. I could find a welcome in the larger inclusive family of faith. Even though I did not continue within the Mennonite church, I have maintained friendships and contacts with individuals within this wonderful organization and have supported efforts to help bring inclusion of gay individuals within the church.

Keith and I continued to visit each for several months but since neither Keith or I felt it was right for us to move to the others' community, we decided in May of 1990 to bring our special relationship as a couple to a close but to continue to be friends. He had such a vital role in my coming out but it was clear to us we were not to be life partners.

Jennifer came home from the university on Spring Break in 1990. I invited her to my new apartment one afternoon so we could talk about how she was feeling about my being gay and the problems it was causing.

Jennifer and I had always been fairly close. We had many discussions about church and social issues. In her last year of high school, she chose to write an essay for a class at school in which she took the position that the church should be more accepting and inclusive of gay people. She knew I was in favor of inclusiveness of gays because of our acceptance of our friend Art in our small group at church. She knew and liked him as well. Jennifer asked me for some suggestions for her paper and I gave her some. She said it was not well received by many in her class.

But this is an entirely different matter now. Her own father was "one of them." It was personal and poignant. It involved *our* family. And she was aware of the struggle her mother was going through after learning about me being gay. Naturally she would be concerned for her mom.

As the time got closer for Jennifer to arrive that afternoon I felt very anxious and vulnerable. Afraid. Would she be angry and disown me? Might she say she never wanted to speak to me again?

I had told myself several weeks before that if my children would refuse to see me because of my being gay, I would return home to Carolyn, if she would have me, and just stay married to keep from breaking up the family. I would somehow try to sublimate my needs and feelings and just exist. Yet I know if I had done that, something beautiful and loving inside me would have died likely resulting in an empty depression. I may not have actually returned home but I am glad I never had to make that painful choice.

After taking off her coat and some general chit chat about her trip home from college, Jennifer sat on the counter between my kitchen and living room, facing me. Her legs dangled down from the counter. I was across the room in a chair fidgeting nervously.

At one point she held up her left hand, looked at me directly and said, "Dad, it's like this. I have dad over here" and then she held up her right hand and said, "and I have gay over here, and I just can't bring the two together yet. I know that I eventually will and I will be fine with it, but it will take some time".

I felt a huge sigh of relief. My worst fears had not come true. I looked at Jennifer and said, "I have had Jim on the one hand over here, and gay on the other hand for forty plus years, and I still have not brought them together completely. So, I understand. Please take whatever time you need. I understand if you are angry and upset by what has happened."

She and I both relaxed more after that was said. She then said, "Dad, the scariest thought I have had about you being gay is that one day in the future, I will likely be married and maybe have a little girl, and I would have to say to that little girl, "Come on Sally, get ready—we are going to see grandpa and his partner." We both chuckled and I said I appreciated her sharing that fear.

I told Jennifer I could understand if she is angry with me for all the problems caused by my coming out. I invited her to write me an angry letter if she felt mad at me. She said she would think about doing so. And, she did. Several weeks later, after she was back in school, I did get her angry letter—and it was not pretty. She gave me a blast and vented her anger.

Her letter was very direct and honest. Even though it was very difficult to read what she wrote, I felt positive that she could tell me how she felt at that time. Naturally, she was feeling a lot for her mother and the pain I caused her mom by my coming out and moving out. In her letter, she tried to be somewhat understanding of what was going on with me.

I also had several talks with my son, Leif, and was amazed at his maturity and ability to speak his mind and feelings at age sixteen. I sensed it was important for he and I to have a talk so I came to the house. Since Carolyn was there, I suggested we go to his bedroom to talk.

When we got to his room, which was amazingly clean, he sat on his brown carpeted floor and I sat on his single bed. He had on his loose fitting sweat shirt and jeans. He looked sad and upset.

I said, "Leif, can you tell me what you are feeling?" He looked down and to the side and then said, "I know you are gay and all but I just can't see where you get off on being married and having a friend on the side!"

I was stunned and quiet. After a moment, I replied, "I know this breaks the rules of being married and what you and I were taught about marriage. This has been most difficult for me and it is why your mom and I are considering divorce." He nodded.

And then said. "And another thing, I don't want you to come back home again. I am afraid it won't work out and mom will get hurt all over again! I don't think a gay man should be married because it is dishonest."

I looked at Leif and said, "I understand your concerns and know you are right in what you just said. Your mom and I are working to sort out what is best for all of us. I appreciate your being honest with me about your thoughts." At that point I rose to leave and Leif stood up as well.

For some reason, I cannot honestly remember if we hugged as I left or not. I don't think we did. I was quite stressed and felt great sadness inside. I did feel we had an honest exchange and that felt very good even though it was painful to hear his concerns.

Coming out to my parents and siblings took place in June of 1990. That was stressful for them and myself. I visited my parents in their house trailer, which was on my brother's farm near Kidron, Ohio. Both listened as I explained what I had been struggling with since childhood. Both tried to be understanding. They could hear the pain in my voice and see my distress as I struggled to say the words.

The next day I wrote in my journal:

Mother was concerned about what the Bible says about homosexuality. But, she also said that she guessed we would have to consider looking at things differently now. She said she has read some about homosexuality in the church papers but never thought our family would be affected by that. She said she loved me and that her far greater concern was with my belief in Christ rather than my homosexual feelings. Mom seemed to have some understanding of homosexuality as genetic predisposition. She asked some questions about me having male friends and asked if they were Christians.

Dad was accepting and warm. He said I was still his son and that he loved me and that he did not believe that Jesus or God would reject me because of being homosexual. Dad seemed to accept that I did not choose to be homosexual. He said, "Jim, you did not do anything wrong, its not like you murdered someone or something.

I felt a big load had been lifted off of me. I felt raw and tender inside like after surgery. Something very deep was released in coming out to mom and dad, they had the privilege of meeting their gay son for the first time. And that gay son could say hello to his parents!

After talking to my parents, I wrote a letter to my siblings and sent it out so they would all find out at the same time. Part of what I said in the letter was:

Dear Family, by now, all of you know that Carolyn and I are separated and have heard that I am gay. One of the main reasons we are apart, but not the only one, is that I have come to accept myself as a man who is gay. Coming to this acceptance has been a very long and very painful process. It has involved years of gradually peeling back the rigid defenses I had constructed to hide this from myself and others. I had to confront my own prejudices and homophobia. It has also involved my choosing to act on and live out what I was discovering about myself. Yesterday, I shared with mother and dad about my situation, including that I was homosexual.

My siblings had planned a family reunion for June, several months before this startling news came to them. I knew the reunion would be awkward, but I also wanted to just be there and just be myself without whispering and rumors going around.

The family reunion went as well as could be expected, given the circumstances. I talked briefly with various family members about the letter I sent but we did not dwell on it. I felt a welcome even though some felt the need to say they did not understand or agree with what I was doing in separating from Carolyn and the children. Of course they knew Carolyn and my kids very well and were very concerned about their well being. I did not expect my siblings to understand or agree with what I was doing and so it was not a huge issue.

Chapter Fourteen

Finding Spirituality

I started attending a Unity church in Akron, Ohio in 1988. I was drawn to their use of quiet meditation in their worship services. They taught meditation classes and focused on the Presence of Christ within each of us. I was welcomed in this church as an out gay man. In time, I was asked to lead meditations and give the homily when the regular minister was away. This church was a breath of fresh air to me. It was such a sharp contrast to the rigid, moralistic religious training I had as a youth. Their teachings helped me make a transition to a more inward and personal spiritual life on my own.

I have experienced that in times of crisis and change in my life journey, I have felt the presence of a Spirit Guide that has spoken words of wisdom and affirmation to me that seem to come from somewhere else. Perhaps it was in those times I was more poignantly in touch with the original authentic self that was my birthright.

It was a very cold Sunday morning in February of 1990, the winter winds were howling and temperatures were below zero. I had just moved out on my own. I decided to go to a gay bath in town instead of church that morning. I had been to this bath a few times before and knew that there was a large dry sauna room which I liked, particularly on very cold days.

After paying my fee, getting a towel and putting my clothes in a locker, I went to the dry sauna room. I was not looking to meet anyone and preferred to be alone. Fortunately there were only a few people in the whole bathhouse and no one else was in the sauna room. No one came in for the twenty minutes I was there.

I lay on the cedar boards on my back and felt the heat penetrating my body. It felt so wonderful—almost two hundred degrees Fahrenheit on a cold blustery morning! It felt so good. I took deep breaths and relaxed so completely I almost fell asleep. I was in a twilight state of awareness.

As I lay there I started to let go of the rigid ego sense of who I was and what I was supposed to be to please others. I began to let myself be ok with being in my body as it was without apology or guilt. My body had a wisdom and truth that I had been trying to ignore and repress. Why not surrender and just let it be? Why not listen honestly to my body?

As I lay there, I realized several very important truths. This entire drama I was playing out in my life certainly had to do with sex, but underneath, at the core, it was not really about sex. It was an odd revelation to have inside a gay bath sauna.

Instead the conflicts I felt were about being comfortable in my body. It was about being able to relax and be as I was as a man. It was about being a good enough man and not a perfect one. It was really about being able to feel what I truly felt rather than what I was supposed to feel. It was about being able to say what was so for me rather than recite the script handed to me. It was about relating to my inner self as a friend and not an enemy. This was a huge revelation and life changing. I could trust the Spirit alive in me.

A few days before this visit to the bath, I had been thinking of the frequency of my own sexual activity. At times it seemed compulsive, both the looking for partners on the internet and the activity itself.

As I lay there in the sauna, I realized that for me the compulsive sexual activity was driven in part by self rejection and self hatred. It became a way in which I tried to get reassurance that I was loveable. If enough men found me desirable maybe I could be convinced I was ok. Of course, that proof was never there. More sex was always needed.

Another very important awareness came to me that morning as I lay in the dry sauna. At the core, this whole drama was not about morality. It was shocking for me to think that this was so. Morality and sex were always linked together in my upbringing. The old black/white, good/bad, right/wrong, sex/dirty paradigms were dissolving. Sex and instinctual energy was no longer bad or evil per se. It seemed sacrilegious to be having these thoughts. But I knew what I was sensing was true.

I lay there on my back covered only by my towel, a few warm tears trickled down the side of my face. Then in front of me I saw a beautiful image of an earthy and compassionate Jesus looking at me with outstretched arms. I noticed his eyes were kind and his smile friendly. He was reaching out to me with love and acceptance. I saw him with the eyes of my being, not with my physical eyes. I did not hear any physical sounds but with my heart I heard him say, "Its Okay, Jim! Just be who you are, as I made you. I love you!"

I put the towel over my face and wept with joy. At first I tried to hold back the tears but soon just yielded to the moment. I took very long, slow, deep cleansing breaths. At the end of the heaving exhale I held my breath—motionless—for what seemed like several minutes, and then began the inhalation again. I felt I was being cleansed from the inside. I felt the calm peacefulness I have sometimes felt when I was clearly and simply myself. I fell asleep for about ten minutes and then awakened. I was awe-struck about what had happened. There was a kind of fear that comes from not fully comprehending what had happened. It was mysterious. I was truly intimate with myself, my inner being and did not want to be intimate with anyone else at that moment. I soon left the bath to return to my apartment.

Back home, I was perplexed about what I had experienced. Could this really be? Was Jesus' presence really there with me that cold winter morning and telling me he was ok with me just as I am. Wasn't he in church either that morning, I chuckled?

I could hardly think of anyone who would believe me, particularly anyone of faith. But I knew that did not matter. My doubt gave way to trust. That presence was like the Jesus I read about in scripture who welcomed the poor and rejected in society, who asked Zacchaeus, a despised tax collector, to come down from his tree and dine. Was He truly saying I did not need to change to be accepted by Him? That He loved me just as He made me? I answered with a resounding " YES!"

Was it Jesus or not? I choose to stop the arguing with myself. If I had been raised in a Muslim culture, the image would likely have been that of Muhammad. Or if I had been raised Jewish, it might have been one of the prophets. And if I had been raised in an Oriental culture, it likely would have appeared as the Buddha or Krishna. But for me being raised in Western culture, the image of Jesus was meaningful and precious.

So I affirmed the reality of a Presence that was with me that morning, a loving, compassionate presence. I was sure that most everyone would think this was blasphemy, meeting Jesus in a gay sauna! I projected that others would think I had really gone off the deep end. But I had been learning not to live by other's beliefs.

In his book *God On Your Own*, Joseph Dispenza talks of finding our innocence in our search for spirituality. He says:

"It means going back to the garden, where life is not seen as a struggle between good and evil but simply is – perfect and in no need of improvement. To be innocent means adopting an attitude that not only is nonjudgmental but goes the next step to believe that people and situations are basically whole and complete just the way they are."

This is exactly what I found that day in the sauna, my innocence and acceptance of my body the way it is. This experience helped me love and accept myself. I learned that spirituality is the awareness of the Compassionate Presence that allows me to love myself and my fellowman. My suffering started to end the moment I stopped resisting the truth and wisdom of my body and its innocence.

* * * * *

In the late summer of 1990, my mother had a stroke and nearly died. However, she did survive but had to be cared for in a nursing home. The family chose a nursing home that also had an assisted living section in Holmes County, Ohio. It was a beautiful facility operated by conservative Mennonites. Because the facility offered assisted living, my father could stay in a one-room apartment and be close to my mother.

I had always felt my dad was loving and compassionate but I did not discover just how much this was true until one beautiful day in August, 1990.

The sun was shining and the sky was blue. I picked up Dad at the assisted living/nursing home complex where mom and dad were living since mom's stroke. I drove the short distance to Sugarcreek, in the heart of Amish Country.

Dad and I boarded a steam engine train that took tourists on a one-hour scenic trip into the Amish countryside. This was where my dad grew up as a boy. I had looked forward to a peaceful and relaxing ride with dad. Unfortunately, the tour leader thought he was a comedian and kept a non-stop stream of puns and anecdotes blaring over the speaker. Many of his puns had sexual innuendos. Some of the jokes might have been funny if told properly. Dad and I were able to talk some on the train even with this distraction.

My grandfather, Gideon Helmuth, was raised Amish but left that faith and joined the Mennonite church so my dad was raised Mennonite. Dad spoke High German or what was called "Pennsylvania Dutch" when a child but also learned English in his 8 years of schooling.

"Dad", I said, "how did you and your dad, Gideon, get along?"

"Well James, Gid had a roofing business and was away a lot. We also raised pigs and butchered them. I had to help with the pigs as well as the cows."

"But how did he treat you?" I asked.

Dad, who seldom said anything negative about anyone, thought a minute, teared up a little and then said,

"I often said, my dad was kinder to the bums who stopped at our farm home for food than he was to his own children."

"What do you mean?" I asked.

"Gid would take these bums in, give them a home cooked meal, let them sleep over night in our home and then sometimes loaned them money as they left in the morning. They never paid him back. They just told other bums where to get food and money."

"Did Gid help you out too?" I asked. Dad said,

"My dad was more tight with his money with us children. He loaned and gave so much to help others he didn't have much left for us. I always felt we were not as important to him as other people. Since we were Helmuths, it was ok if we did without. I think it was more important for Gid to look good to others."

Dad continued, "but my dad did help us some when it was time for us to move out or when we children got married."

When Dad and I returned, we sat in my white 1989 Pontiac Grand Prix overlooking the beautiful farmland and countryside of Holmes County, with its green pastures and perfectly manicured fields of corn and wheat.

Dad and I sat there and talked for over an hour. Dad said,

"Jim, I have had doubts about what happens after death. And I don't think anyone knows for sure. Eventually we will find out when we die. But I have decided I can have a better life living by the church's teachings and if the teachings are wrong, I will still be better off having believed and lived accordingly."

I said, "Dad, I am surprised to hear you say you have doubts also. I feel closer to you now because of my own doubts and struggles to believe. But, I can't pretend to believe something that I don't. And so I have chosen to leave the Mennonite Church. But, I am seeking a spiritual life in other ways."

Dad nodded with understanding. He then asked, "Jim, how do you know for sure you are gay?" I explained that ever since a child I felt different from other boys and as I grew older I found I wanted to be close and intimate with men." Dad listened as I told him about some of my experiences growing up. Then he said,

"There was a Mennonite minister in our community that everyone said was 'funny that way' around the boys and we were warned to be careful when around him." We both chuckled at that.

Dad expressed his misgivings about what I was doing in leaving Carolyn. I heard his concerns. I did not feel though that dad was judging me. He just said what he was thinking and feeling. How I wish dad and I had been able to talk openly like that years earlier.

Before we parted, I turned to dad and said, " You know dad, when I knew for sure I was gay, I was tempted to move to a big city where I could hide like many gay guys do. But, I wanted to stay close to my family and remain part of it if I could. So, instead I decided to try to live my life honestly as a gay man right here in our area and to come to our family reunions."

Dad said, "James, your mom and I appreciate that you did not run away but kept in contact with our family." He grasped my hand and with tears in his eyes and a halting voice added, "James, I love you. You were always a special son to your mother and I. More than anything we want you to be happy in life and open to what God has for you."

I grasped my dad's hand in return and said, "Dad, I love you too. I appreciate just how much you shared with me today and for accepting me as I am." After getting out of the car, we had a heartfelt, long embrace. It was at that moment I felt a bond between my soul and dad's, and felt healing in our relationship. The anger I had felt toward him for not being there for me when

I was growing up was gone. In my most vulnerable moment, he was there for me as the father I needed. We parted and Dad went back to mom's room in the nursing home to have dinner with my mother.

As I drove home that day, there were tears of joy. I felt the joy of honest, direct communication, absent of judging and pretense. It was so good to say what I honestly felt instead of what I should believe or feel. It was good to start with my body, listen to its truth and wisdom, learn to trust it and to honor its needs. This has been the learning in my life journey.

Dad was very committed to providing for us six children and raising us in the church. We farmed a 100 acre farm and had thousands of chickens. To help "make ends meet," dad worked four or five days a week driving a meat delivery truck to Cleveland. He would leave the house at 2 a.m. and sometimes not get home until 6 or 7 p.m.

Sometimes I got to go with dad when he worked on a Saturday. He would also take me fishing sometimes on a weekend. I didn't like fishing that much, but I liked being with my dad. He loved hunting and fishing and had a great appreciation for nature. He would love to go in the woods in the fall and sit quietly under a tree to wait for squirrels. Dad was soft spoken and very kind. But he also had a temper if pushed too far and I knew just where that line was and seldom challenged it.

At Dad's funeral, there was a time for anyone to share thoughts and memories about dad. One of my cousins, Galen, who had lived with us for a period of time while he was growing up, went to the microphone. The only thing I remember he said was that my father "was the kindest man I ever knew." My heart resonated with that simple truth.

* * * * *

In February of 1990, I responded to an ad in the *Gay People's Chronicle*. The Chronicle is a Cleveland and Akron area gay-owned newspaper that had articles of interest to gay people. It also provided a place for gays to meet other gays through personal ads. In browsing the ads I came upon this one:

Akron GWM, 47,6', 160#, brown hair, mustache, professional, sincere, caring, friendly, horny, fun-loving, straight-acting, social drinker, non-smoker, no drugs. Seeks same 30 – 50 for friendship, physical relationship. Enjoys conversation, movies. Box #274.

I was very interested. I liked that he described himself as "professional, sincere, fun-loving and horny." I also liked that he wanted friendship and enjoyed conversation. So, on Feb. 15th, 1990 I wrote:

Dear # 274, Hi, My name is Jim. I am 46, 5'9 and 157 lbs. I have a short beard and moustache and curly brown hair. I could have written your ad myself in that your descriptors of you and what your interests are fit me quite well. I am looking for friendship and male bonding, including good safe sex. I am open to a committed relationship but in no hurry at this time. I am gentle and sensitive.

I wrote a few other things and included my phone number. I sent my letter to the Chronicle and they forwarded it to Rich. I did not get a response for about a week and then he called, said he was responding to my ad and his name was Rich. He left his phone number on my answer machine.

I was curious he called himself "Rich" rather than Richard or Dick. Later he told me that "Rich" was his gay name. It is how he referred to himself when introducing himself to other gay men.

He and I left messages on each other's answer machines over several days. I thought this was not going to go any place. It seemed he was too busy. But, we did eventually make live phone contact and agreed on a meeting time and place.

Chapter Fifteen

April Fools

It was Sunday, April 1, 1990. I went to the Unity church which was located in west Akron at that time. I was nervous during the service as I was thinking about the planned meeting at 1:00 p.m. I was to meet "Rich," a guy I had talked with on the phone only once after reading his ad in a gay newspaper. He invited me to his place in west Akron. He told me he was a church organist but would be home by 12:30 p.m.

I rushed home from my church, ate a sandwich, brushed my teeth, spritzed on cologne, gargled mouthwash, primped my hair and left for the encounter. I was very nervous as I pulled in the driveway of Rich's ranch style home and walked up the walkway to the front door. The house had wood siding that was painted a medium blue, with light yellow shutters. It was surrounded with overgrown shrubbery. It definitely needed a makeover.

I was nervous meeting someone like me, a gay man who had a professional career. This was the kind of guy I was looking for. Otherwise I knew nothing about this "Rich". Perhaps I sensed something good might be about to happen. How could I have known that this was the start of twenty years of a wonderful, loving relationship? How could I have even dreamed that the man who would come to that door that day would become my very best friend, my confidant, my travel guide and my lover?

There he was, tall, lanky and smiling nervously but broadly. He invited me in. I could tell Rich was as nervous as I was as he sat on the ugly gray couch he kept from his divorce. The couch was on a right angle from the love seat, where I sat.

We checked each other out, asking about jobs and family. He had been married for twenty-five years and had two sons. They were just a few years older than my son and daughter. He said his wife had divorced him about two months earlier because she wanted her own life.

Rich said he taught organ, keyboard skills and music theory at The University of Akron for twenty-three years. Since age fifteen, Rich always had a job at some church as an organist or organist/choirmaster. I told him about my family, my coming out and my work as a psychologist.

I also told Rich of my relationship with Keith, from Iowa, but said I did not think it was going to work as neither of us was willing to relocate to the other's community. I also told Rich I had been deliberately abstinent the last six weeks to take a break from the gay dating scene and to give me time to sort out what was next for me..

Soon Rich came over to the love seat and sat aside of me. We held hands and gently touched each other. I always teased Rich that he seduced me and it is partly true since he took the initiative that day. He claims it was the opposite. And there is some truth in that as well. It was completely mutual. In the horse race between fear and passion, passion was winning by a mile.

Early on Rich asked if I was sure I wanted to continue the intimacy since I had been abstinent for 6 weeks. It was very considerate of him to ask. I said I was sure that I did, so we continued in his bedroom. That day a spark of love was ignited that has continued to grow and glow within us through the years. Our relationship has gone through the usual phases and changes all relationships go through as they mature.

I started getting cards, flowers and phone calls from Rich almost every day. I accepted all of what was offered and reciprocated in kind. We loved hiking together through various parks in our area. Each of us continued to date a few other men for a while even though we were spending more and more time together.

On our first hike in the Gorge Park in Akron, we discovered that we both liked to go to gourmet restaurants. We started making of list of restaurants we would like to go to together. If there wasn't an obvious holiday to celebrate, we could always invent something for each occasion. Not that we needed to have a special occasion. Each time we met we were celebrating our new found love and friendship and it was wonderfully special.

Six weeks after meeting Rich, I wrote in my journal:

Now comes Rich, ending my abstinence of 6 weeks! The feelings were strong and clear from the beginning. There is a positive chemistry between us on several levels. One is the physical/sexual. He is attractive to me and he shows that I am to him. When we touch, I am aroused in a way that is unique. I am moved very deeply by it and sometimes feel tears of joy. I experience feelings of bonding and love that are deep and genuine. I long to be with him and miss him when we are apart.

He is mature, responsible, confident, gentle, humorous, talented and caring. I respect his abilities immensely. He does not try to control or manipulate me in certain directions. He accepts me as I am and lets me be who I am. I do not have any urges to change him in any basic way. Where did I find such a one? Was I digging in a diamond mine and found one? I must be doing something right to be led to this very special friend.

Five months after we met, Rich had a family reunion in California that was planned a year before. He was scheduled to be away for 16 days, and it would be our first time apart.

I was quite stressed to have Rich gone for so long so early in our relationship. Somewhere I found tiny two inch by two inch cards in small envelopes with a mint candy inside each. I put a number from one to sixteen on the outside of each, one for each of sixteen days we would be apart. Inside each was several sentences describing a special time we had shared since we met, like a special dinner or a creative and spontaneous activity that we did together.

I hid this card set in his suitcase with the instructions that he was to open one each day and remember that event as he ate the mint. I had a list of the events at home so I could think of the same one on that day. Rich was delighted with this creative way of being present with each other while absent and it helped us get through this first separation.

I was feeling love and care for Rich but had some difficulty letting him get as close to me as he wanted. After all, the walls and defenses I built over the years to protect myself from rejection were thick and high. They do not come down easily even with reassurances.

Three months after we met, we hiked again in the Gorge Park. After our hike that day we stopped at the Liberty Brewing Company in the Merriman

Valley of Akron for a bite to eat. This was one of those micro breweries that were popular then and their home made fresh brews were refreshing.

As we waited for our food, Rich reached his hand across the table, grasped my hand, looked me in the eye and said, "Jim, I love you very much, and I am sure I want us to always be together as partners. You are the right one for me!". What a moment. Time stopped. Was this really happening to me? What do I do? What do I say? My mind was racing.

I glanced away then looked back at Rich. "I love you very much as well," I said, "but, I am just not as certain that you are the best partner for me for ever. And even more, I am not sure it is ok for me to let anyone love me as much as you say you do! Can we give it some time to let our relationship grow?" He looked a little disappointed, but said, "Sure lets give it time and see what happens."

At some level I was not sure anyone who really knew me could truly love me. How could I ever risk that? If I could not trust my own family and friends with my secrets, how could I risk letting a person I just met several months ago know me and love me? I presumed that since I did not fully love and accept myself, certainly no one else could either.

Groucho Marx reportedly said, "I would never join a club that would have me as a member." Exactly. I was so convinced my gay self was shameful and unlovable that it was difficult to believe anyone could love me. I was afraid of love, afraid of being loved, afraid to trust my tender heart to anyone. What I longed for and waited for all my life was there. Could I accept it?

What I was finding in my life was that the more I was good, kind and fair to myself, the more kind and loving I could be with Rich and others. The more I learned to soothe and nurture myself when feeling down or lonely, the less risky it was to allow Rich to love me intimately.

One issue Rich and I had to negotiate was the amount of time together. Rich was very busy with his teaching schedule at The University of Akron, half time church job and requests for accompanying performers at recitals. Did he have time for a relationship? He was struggling to make time for us, but it was always clear he genuinely wanted to do so. I needed to learn patience and trust. I had my own private practice and activities but they did not take up as much free time as Rich's. This concern did get better after Rich retired from the university and had more free time.

My self hatred and distrust was changing slowly. Coming out to my family helped immensely. And now as Rich showed me in so many wonderful ways that he truly did love me, I began to respond and trust him.

Rich and I had many fun times hiking and going to the Headlands Beach along Lake Erie that summer. Since I was in private practice and he had some days free after teaching, we could plan afternoons and evenings together. We started to talk about vacationing together over the winter holidays. I recall feeling very uneasy planning 3 months ahead because I was not sure we would still be together yet at that time. Rich was understanding and patient. How could he be so sure and I be so unsure? It was me I was unsure of.

Rich and I spent a week at my time-share condo in Cancun in January of 1991. We got to know each other much better that week and our friendship deepened. The intensity of our intimacy confused and excited me. I was confused because it was new and very powerful. And yet it was exciting. Trust was building the more we were together.

In Cancun, Rich's favorite place was relaxing in the beautiful outdoor connecting pools at the condominium resort. One pool had a bar on the one side so one could sit on stools submerged in the water and sip margaritas or other cocktails.

One day while we were sitting there, Rich asked me if I would move in with him at his home in July after his son got married. I was excited and delighted that he asked but was taken by surprise. I had to think about it. I wanted to say yes right away, but knew I was not ready yet to make that commitment.

Rich's ex-wife had asked him for a divorce before she knew he was gay. They had grown apart and she wanted to pursue a new career in the ministry. He had not come out yet to anyone in his family. I was adamant that I had not left my closet only to go into his. It would be a step back for me.

Rich understood my concern but was very scared to come out to his family. I also was concerned about his overly busy schedule with university teaching, church job and accompanying. We did break up for a two week period to give me some time to reconsider our relationship. That really helped clarify my feelings for Rich. I could hardly hold out the two week agreement. I think we cut it short by several days and decided to talk.

I was wavering about following through with dissolution of my marriage. I knew I had to do it but kept trying to find some way to return home. Carolyn and I had only been separated for twelve months.

Rich and I made an agreement that within six months, I would agree to come to a resolution of my marriage situation and he would find a way to come out to his family. But things proceeded even more quickly on his part. Rich came out to his ex wife and sons within the next two or three months after our agreement. And soon after that he came out to his siblings.

Our relationship got back on track. Rich and I began seeing each other almost daily. He recalls having "bell practice" with his handbell choir at his church on Thursday evenings. He would finish the rehearsal right on the dot and dash out the door, get in his car and make a beeline for my apartment. He always wondered if the ladies were curious where he was going in such a hurry. If they only knew!

During that first year away from my family, I continued to talk with Carolyn periodically about the possibly of returning home and making it work between us. That longing to return came from a deep resistance to divorcing. I was also grieving the loss of my "ideal" family unit and the marriage. It was a very deep grief and I just needed time to work through the process. I felt deep emotional pain. I did love Carolyn very much.

It is hard to overstate the intensity of conflicted feelings I had about ending my relationship with Carolyn. She and I had many hours of honest, gut wrenching sharing about our feelings for each other and our feelings about what was happening in our life situation. We even considered how it might work for me to return home and me still maintain a relationship with Rich. Maybe I could have both. That was one of the dumbest ideas we ever discussed.

That kind of arrangement did not really make sense for us as neither Carolyn nor I could go on with our lives. I wrote self dialogues and letters in my journal to help process my feelings.

At one point it seemed that Carolyn and I were just rehashing feelings and it wasn't going anywhere. I wrote a poem during this time that shows the conflict between feeling very deep love for Carolyn that was there and yet the awareness of the absence of the erotic love and bonding that was not there and would not likely ever be there.

After one four hour marathon sharing session, Carolyn and I did come to the conclusion that the best thing was for us to start a process of dissolution of our marriage. Over the summer of 1991, we worked with a Social Worker/ Attorney who drew up the agreement Carolyn and I had worked out on our own. The divorce hearing was September 6, 1991 at 8:15 a.m. It took about ten minutes of court time in front of a magistrate. It seemed so easy. But it was perhaps one of the most difficult things I have ever done. I want to be clear, the problem was not with Carolyn, the problem was that I, a gay man, was heterosexually married and therein is a fundamental conundrum.

The day after Rich's oldest son's wedding, I moved into Rich's three bedroom ranch home. I preferred for us to buy a place together so it would be ours. But, Rich wanted to stay at the home, as he had just refinanced and the location was ideal.

I agreed to stay there and over the years we have remolded every room in the house to make it ours. The outside was completely re-landscaped. We also added a beautiful patio and a perennial garden out the back with a path leading back to a secluded vine covered swing. Each year I add annual flowers to the perennials to make a gorgeous setting for parties and our own use.

Often now, on a Sunday morning, I love to go out and get good quality fresh ingredients to bring home to make a special dinner for Rich. Especially on winter mornings I love putting a roast and vegetables in the slow cooker and letting it cook and create its wonderful aroma in the whole house until ready to eat about four p.m.

Because I prepare this food with my heart, this simple act nourishes not only Rich and our relationship but also myself. It has a totally different meaning than just making food to gobble up. Rich has come to appreciate this part of our relationship very much.

Typically, we will have a cocktail drink and appetizer before our meal and we take time to enjoy our time together. We are present with each other as we share the meal, without distractions. We talk about the past week and make some plans for the next. It has become something of a ritual but each time is different.

I have had difficulty understanding the meaning of the Eucharist in the Episcopal or any other church, which I have attended periodically in the last eight years. But just having written about sharing food and a meal in an intimate way with a loved one, perhaps this is getting close to what the Eucharist is all about and why Jesus reportedly asked his followers to "sit at table" together to remember him. I have been attending the gay-affirming Church of Our Saviour, Episcopal Church here in Akron, Ohio. While I do not connect so much with the rituals of organized religion, I do appreciate the love and support our church extends to all people including those of different sexual orientations.

* * * * *

When I met Rich, I met a man who loved to travel. He had many trips to Europe for school and sabbaticals. Fortunately, I loved to travel as well and so we took many trips together over the years. Rich is, by his own admission, "anal retentive". That means he likes to save and count things. He has calendars of our life together since we first met. I asked him to list all the trips he and I took together outside of Ohio. The number came to fifty-three in the twenty years we have been together. These included a number of trips to Mexico for vacations but also trips to some parts of Europe. Traveling together has enriched our lives greatly and has given us a wealth of wonderful memories.

In 2005, we celebrated fifteen years together. We rented a party center and invited friends and relatives. It was a grand occasion with about eighty people in attendance. Of course there was an open bar and we had lots of our favorite foods and appetizers. A friend made a great cake for us. We made a grand entrance in our tuxedos with lots of cheers and whistles.

We had beautiful instrumental music during the evening. There was a short ceremony of celebration. My oldest brother, David, who is a Mennonite minister, read a scripture passage. Megan, the rector from Church of Our Saviour Episcopal, where Rich is organist/choirmaster, gave a short meditation.

Rich and I then read a responsive dialogue which I had written for the occasion:

CELEBRATION !

Jim: This day we proudly celebrate our relationship of 15 years.

Rich: Over these years, our relationship has grown from friendship and romance to a deeper loving and caring. The love we feel for each other has been enduring and joyful beyond words.

Jim: We have often been in awe at the way our different interests and abilities have fit together....like two pieces of a puzzle. When we are together, we are at home with ourselves and feel complete and whole. And when we are apart, we feel that part of us is missing and looks forward to reuniting.

Rich: In those perfect moments of joy, like when we are in a beautiful setting in nature, or eating a special meal by our fireplace, one of us will invariable say "TITL" —T-I-T-L—and the other readily agrees—"**This Is The Life!**"

Jim: We have enjoyed traveling together to many cities and countries, from A to Z—Amsterdam to Zoar—and many places in between. These travels have enriched our relationship and life together.

Rich: Our relationship has defied time, the differences in our personalities and the many changes in ourselves and life situations. This love we celebrate today has nurtured our inner and outer lives in countless ways.

Jim: As threads are woven together to make a cloth....each one of you has in some way helped support and nurture our life together. And for this we are deeply grateful.

Together: **Today we celebrate this gift of love—and boldly proclaim our intention—to continue loving each other—throughout our lives.**

This responsive reading captures the breadth and depth of our relationship. But it is clearly not only about us. Rich has two adult sons and I have an adult son and a daughter. Over the years, they have met and been with each other at holiday times at our place. They all seem to like each other and get along very well.

Chapter Sixteen

Another Birth

In August of 2004, Rich and I took all our children and their spouses on a one week cruise up Alaska's Inside Passage. It was a wonderful way for all of our children to get to know each other even better. Every evening we would meet for dinner and tell what excursions or activities we had experienced that day. We feel so blessed to have children and now grandchildren who love and accept us as we are.

Many people feel uneasy around gay people, particularly if they do not know any out gay people as friends or relatives. Others rail against the evils of the gay lifestyle and warn about how gays would destroy marriage if allowed to marry. Some spread lies based on ignorance, fear and prejudice.

I wonder if these individuals who fear or even despise gay people could let themselves experience the kind of love we have in our family and other families with gay parents and children, they might come to see that their focus on the sex aspect of being gay was and is totally misguided and wrong. It is they who are obsessed with sex. They might have to see the awful truth that it is they who have often made sexual behavior the issue and not gay people.

I love the story of the monks who were chaste and celibate. They were to be so pure they ideally were not to even notice a lady was a lady. One day as they walked to the temple there was a lady mired in mud, trying to cross the stream. One monk reached out and helped carry her across the stream.

His self-righteous brother was so bothered and angered by this he could not think of anything else while trying to meditate that day. So that evening, he confronted his brother about it saying "You should not have done that, you should not even have noticed that lady, you were wrong!" The other monk replied, "I carried her across the stream once today. You have been carrying her across all day!"

* * * * *

The week after we returned from Alaska, I had an appointment with my family doctor for a check up. I had been noticing that I was not able to be on the treadmill as long as previously without having some shortness of breath. I did not, however, have chest pain or numbness.

My doctor listened closely and suggested that I have a cardiolite stress test just to be sure it wasn't anything serious. I agreed it would be good to check it out so the next Wednesday I had the test.

After the test, the nurse suggested that I take a break and get some lunch and then come back for the results. When I returned the nurse reported that they had talked to my family doctor and he wanted me to talk with a cardiologist before I left. They said a cardiologist would see me shortly.

The cardiologist looked at my test result and said a heart catheterization was needed to find out what was going on. He made a few calls and within an hour he did the catheterization.

The cardiologist saw that four arteries were blocked and recommended quadruple bypass surgery. He advised me to stay in the hospital as they could do the bypass in two days. It was obvious something was very wrong.

This came as a huge shock to Rich and my family. Rich had to call and cancel my appointments and email my family and friends. It was a very scary thing for him and my family. My daughter and her husband came down from Canada.

Amazingly, I felt a calm peacefulness throughout the preparation and the morning of the surgery. I felt happy that we had taken this great cruise to Alaska and that I had so many wonderful times with Rich. I was ready to die if the operation did not go well. I was so happy that I had lived my life fully and had found the joy of living honestly.

The operation was successful. I was released from the hospital in about five days. It's been five years since the CABG and I have made a full recovery.

I go to the gym regularly and work out for sixty to ninety minutes. I take brisk hikes in the park and my energy level is good. My doctor says I probably have the best lipid profile in Summit County.

I did have to do some thinking about my life choices and whether I wanted to continue doing psychotherapy. I decided that I loved the work I was doing and that I did want to continue at least for a few more years. But, I did not want to see as many clients in a day. I started taking more time in the evenings to walk in my garden and enjoy the flowers. I love watching the wild birds that come to the feeder. I wanted to take more vacations. And that is exactly what I am doing.

One of the payoffs of having made the choice to live my life honestly and do the hard work of healing my inner pain, is that I have no regrets. I can come to the end of my life with a sense of fulfillment, peace and joy.

A very special joy I experienced the last several years has been to follow my daughter Jennifer's pregnancy and the birth of my grandson, Samuel James Roth. When I learned that Jennifer was pregnant, I wrote this prayer and prayed it until he was born:

"Dear Source of Life, Dear Ground of Being, Dear Instiller of Breath, even now in cellular form, be present in love in the child to be, and bring that seed to full life and form so that it can be filled with the breath of life at birth. Amen."

I have done eight needle point projects over the last 5 years. Most of them have been flowers. I bought a needle point kit of beautiful butterflies to do for my grandchild to be. The six months before Sammy was born I worked on the project stitch by stitch. Just before he was born, I wrote a note to go along with my gift. It said:

"Reflections while working on Butterfly Needlepoint:

It's only days now until your arrival from the comfort of the womb to a different life on this planet earth. While you were being knit together in your mother's womb this summer, I was doing this needle point project stitch by stitch. Sometimes I was watching TV or listening to music and sometimes-just thinking about this gift I was making for you, my first grandchild.

These beautiful butterflies I give to you. They were once in a cocoon also and inwardly forming wings to fly. One day it was just the right time for them to leave their old form, exercise their wings and fly.

You too, my grandchild, come with the inner knowledge of who you uniquely are, why you are here and what you need to do or be in this life. May you find your wings to take you to your highest good. Bless you!"

Grandfather Helmuth

My grandson, Samuel James Roth, was born September 23, 2007. I was elated. Within a few days, Richard and I went to see Sammy in Waterloo, Ontario where my daughter and her husband live.

As soon as we were in their home, Jennifer proudly presented me with Sammy. Holding him in my arms for the first time was an exhilarating and awesome experience. Whatever uneasiness Jennifer had imagined seven years earlier in bringing her child to grandpa and his partner was completely gone. Time and love had woven us together as a family.

After I held Sammy awhile, Rich held him in his long and gentle arms. Sammy fell asleep. Rich held him patiently as Sammy slept soundly for two hours. Evidently Sammy felt at peace with Rich, as do I. The circle of life is complete. Love makes it so.

Afterword

This project of writing this book has been growing inside for a very long time. I started writing a book at least five different times over the last twenty years. Each time I would write some but then not follow through. I think there are several reasons for that.

One reason was that I had such high expectations for any book I would write that I believed I would be disappointed. I also was hesitant because I knew that my writing would involve some disclosure of feelings that were very personal and private. Some of those feelings and life events I had not even fully admitted yet to myself.

In April of 2008 I read a book, *God On Your Own*, by Joseph Dispenza. I identified with what he wrote so closely I contacted him to see about taking his Hero Journey Retreat that he and his colleagues offered at his Life Path Retreat Center in San Miguel de Allende, Mexico. I found Joseph very genuine and open, just as he was in his writings.

In August of 2008, I had a four-day personal retreat with Joseph Dispenza to see if I could remove the block I had to writing. The group retreat I was registered for was postponed but he graciously agreed to work with me one on one. That turned out to be exactly what I needed at that time in my life!

Joseph and I looked at my core values and beliefs. We discussed my fears and insecurities and how those held me back from speaking my truth to the world. He gave me writing exercises to focus my intentions. And he encouraged me to think and develop my life events as movie scenes.

As I worked with Joseph Dispenza I realized that what I really needed was someone who has written books to coach me in the process. I knew that Joseph had written a number of successful books.

I am seldom impulsive and I sometimes have difficulty asking for what I really want and need. But in one of our sessions, I spontaneously asked Joseph if he would be my book coach. At first, he said no. The next morning he told me he thought about it and decided he would be willing to do this. He felt that many other people could benefit from hearing my story of coming out.

My rationale for writing this book is that it has been my experience that there is one particular activity in which truth from the Source is less distorted. That one activity is storytelling.

As we tell our stories of our journey in life, if we consciously reflect on what we are saying, we can get a sense of something unique going on with us. As we honestly tell our stories, some truth and mystery comes forth from the details. Between the clouds of life events floating by we sometimes catch a glimmer of the Sky behind the clouds and can see the beauty of the truth, "it is all good."

I was self-conscious about growing up Mennonite but mostly because it meant I was different from other students. That was my first closet. When at school or out in public I made efforts to conceal being Mennonite by making sure I looked like everyone else and secretly listening to popular music so I knew the tunes. Mennonite girls were supposed to wear longer dresses and hair so it was harder for them to hide if they wanted to.

I don't know how the other students knew I was Mennonite but they did. I would overhear classmates talk about a movie they had seen or about going to a party. One of them would sometimes say, "You aren't allowed to go to movies or dance are you?" I shrugged and said yes, that's how it's supposed to be. But I knew some Mennonite young people were doing both and I myself was able to go to some movies by age fifteen. It helped when our family finally got a small, twelve inch Admiral black and white TV when I was just thirteen.

So, when my writing coach and an editor friend kept asking me to include more stories of growing up Mennonite in this book I was puzzled. "Why include something I have left long ago and no longer believe? I argued. "Because it's interesting and an important part of the context of your life story", they said. And they are right.

I often encouraged my clients to be honest about who they were and to live authentically. Many of them have secret lives and suffer because of it. I would cheer them on as they took steps to be more genuine and honest in relationships. And yet, I myself did not have the courage to follow my own advice until mid life. This book is much more than a coming out gay story. It's about finding and living out of our authentic selves.

After I started writing this book, it seemed my story had a life and energy of its own. I awakened sometimes at 2 a.m. and other times at 5 a.m. with an urge to write down ideas that were in my consciousness. I felt the need to turn off the TV and the Internet so I could express new material that was forming.

Writing this book has itself been a journey for me that nothing else could bring. I have re-visited the very tender and painful parts of my self but also the joyful and loving parts as well.

During my late adolescent years and beyond, part of me knew I was hiding from and ignoring my same sex attraction. I knew I was betraying myself but did not have the courage to face my feelings directly at that time. It seems I had to go down a few roads to see that they led to a dead end. Eventually I did not know who I was anymore and I became more depressed and desperate. I stopped living and just existed. I was not able to really live but not quite able to die. That is, until one spring evening.

We all have a story to tell, a journey of discovery, learning, and the ups and downs of life. Possibly its something we have feared or denied or hidden. Some drama has played out in our every life. We can learn by listening to our own stories and those of others with compassion and understanding.

And so I told my story for those of you who might find, in reading it, strength and encouragement to take responsibility to find your own joy and happiness, to honor your innate wisdom and to live with integrity. I also told it so that my children and grandchildren can learn about what their father/grandfather experienced in his life. Two of my core values are honesty and understanding and I've tried to bring both to this manuscript.

About the Author

Dr. James Helmuth graduated with a B.A. degree in Social Science Comprehensive and Education from Malone College in Canton, Ohio. He earned a Masters Degree in Religion from Earlham School of Religion and a Ph.D. in Guidance and Counseling from The University of Akron, in Akron, Ohio. He is a licensed psychologist in the state of Ohio and owner of Helmuth Psychological Associates in Akron since 1986. He has taught workshops on Stress Management, Dual Diagnosis In Substance Abuse Recovery, Overcoming Depression and Coping with Posttraumatic Stress. In his private practice he treats mood disorders, relationship issues and trauma/anxiety disorders. Dr. Helmuth has done psychological testing and treatment for over three hundred fifty impaired police and firemen in Ohio. He lives in Akron, Ohio with his partner.